Management by Policy

Also available from Quality Press

Integrated Process Management: A Quality Model
Roger Slater

Ethics in Quality
August B. Mundel

Quality Management Benchmark Assessment
J. P. Russell

A Guide to Graphical Problem-Solving Process
John W. Moran, Richard P. Talbot,
and Russell M. Benson

Benchmarking: The Search for Industry Best Practices That Lead to Superior Performance
Robert C. Camp

QFD: A Practitioner's Approach
James L. Bossert

To request a complimentary catalog of publications, call 800-248-1946.

Management by Policy

How Companies Focus Their Total Quality Efforts to Achieve Competitive Advantage

Brendan Collins
Ernest Huge

ASQC Quality Press
Milwaukee, Wisconsin

Management by Policy: How Companies Focus Their Total Quality Efforts to Achieve Competitive Advantage
Brendan Collins
Ernest Huge

Library of Congress Cataloging-in-Publication Data

Collins, Brendan
Management by policy: how companies focus their total quality efforts to achieve competitive advantage / Brendan Collins, Ernest Huge.
p. cm.
Includes bibliographical references and index.
ISBN 0-87389-241-0
1. Total quality management. 2. Management. I. Huge, Ernest C.
II. Title.
HD62.15.C6 1993
658.5'62—dc20 93-16933
CIP

10 9 8 7 6 5 4 3 2 1

ISBN 0-87389-241-0

Acquisitions Editor: Susan Westergard
Production Editor: Annette Wall
Marketing Administrator: Mark Olson
Set in Stone Sans and Goudy by Montgomery Media, Inc.
Cover design by Montgomery Media, Inc.
Printed and bound by BookCrafters, Inc.

ASQC Mission: To facilitate continuous improvement and increase customer satisfaction by identifying, communicating, and promoting the use of quality principles, concepts, and technologies; and thereby be recognized throughout the world as the leading authority on, and champion for, quality.

For a free copy of the ASQC Quality Press Publications Catalog, including ASQC membership information, call 800-248-1946.

Printed in the United States of America.

  Printed on acid-free recycled paper

ASQC
Quality Press
611 East Wisconsin Avenue
Milwaukee, Wisconsin 53202

Contents

Preface

Management by policy (MBP) is a landmark development in the practice of business management. It represents the highest degree to which world-class companies have evolved the application of total quality principles. MBP isn't management theory. It is the way some companies manage today. MBP focuses the company's resources on a few priority issues that provide significant competitive advantage. It works in a way that fosters cooperation, cross-functional support, and a win-win way of doing business.

Does this sound like yet another ill-fated magic bullet? If it doesn't, then what is unique about MBP?

When oil prices soared in 1973, some excellent Japanese companies that exported to the United States didn't pass on the increased energy costs to the U.S. market. Neither did they suffer reduced profits. Instead, they found a way to reduce costs to offset the energy cost increase.

Those companies used management by policy. Since the energy crisis there have been other opportunities for those companies to apply their newly developed MBP capability, as when the Japanese yen's value against the dollar increased drastically. With every one of these opportunities, their MBP capability improved. Although MBP was originally developed as a defensive weapon, it has evolved into a major offensive weapon that the excellent Japanese companies use to obtain and keep market dominance.

In many U.S. companies that purport to have a formal quality management process, quality is just a veneer on existing management techniques. Quality planning is viewed as a subset of strategic business planning. Top managers expect their planning groups to do all of the analysis and to make all of the recommendations from which top management makes the final decision. In contrast, excellent Japanese companies use total quality (TQ) principles to run their businesses. MBP based upon TQ principles is their strategic business planning process. Financial planning follows from MBP. Top managers do the strategic planning themselves. They perform the analysis and identify alternative recommendations. Strategic planning by top managers is viewed as a core competency.

When first exposed to MBP, many people have commented that it's what management by objectives (MBO) was supposed to be—or that, at best, it is nothing but a slight improvement of MBO. Actually, MBP is vastly different from MBO in all dimensions.

Whereas MBO is concerned only with goals, MBP is concerned with goals *and* the means to achieve the goals. In MBP *policy* means both the goal and the means. MBP goals are established only after a thorough analysis of the means and resources—both necessary and available—to achieve the goals.

MBO is driven by financial results; MBP focuses on achieving customer satisfaction, thereby ensuring the attainment of financial goals. MBO is focused on results; MBP on both the process and the results.

Whereas MBO is driven from the top down, MBP is driven from both the top down and the bottom up. MBP considers the input and requires the buy-in of everyone who must execute the plan and achieve the goals. But buy-in isn't enough. The analysis of resources and means must justify and support the goals.

MBO isn't integrated across functional areas, and frequently doesn't connect from the higher to the lower levels of the organization. MBP is tightly integrated horizontally and vertically throughout the organization.

MBO is usually disconnected from an ongoing execution process; MBP involves both planning and execution. With MBO, objectives are frequently determined by gut feelings alone; MBP requires analysis backed by data.

MBO often involves numerous objectives with unclear priorities. MBP establishes clear priorities for the significant few policies that will have the greatest impact. By separating the smoke from the substance, MBP makes the difficult resource trade-off decisions.

Chapters 1 and 2 present total quality—the context for management by policy. Chapter 3 describes what MBP is. Chapter 4 shows how to implement policies. Chapter 5 shows how to implement a management-by-policy system. Chapter 6 concludes with a discussion of the spirit or inherent energy of management by policy.

The purpose of chapters 1 and 2 is to confirm the reader's understanding of TQ and how it is implemented. If you have a thorough understanding of the concepts of TQ, you can proceed immediately to chapter 3. If you do not, you should start with chapter 1. If you know what TQ is but are just beginning implementation, you can proceed to chapter 2, which describes the TQ implementation process.

Chapter 1. Total Quality—The Context of Management by Policy

What is this thing that people call "a new business paradigm"? The body of knowledge is organized into 16 principles.

The primary purpose of chapter 1 is to ensure that you have the prerequisite understanding of total quality. We assume that you are committed to total quality as the way to run a business. No attempt is made to answer the question "Why total quality?"

Chapter 2. Implementing Total Quality

How does a company do it? Is there one way, or are there different approaches? What works? What doesn't? What works best? What are the prerequisites?

Chapter 3. Elements of Management by Policy
MBP is described in terms of three major elements.

1. Developing policies
2. Deploying policies throughout the organization
3. Implementing policy, which involves a continuous review of progress relative to plans and a periodic evaluation of the entire MBP process

A detailed conceptual discussion of each of the elements is given, along with an example.

Chapter 4. Implementing Policy
The essence of policy implementation centers around the systematic application of basic TQ tools. This will ensure that the best solution is found—one that eliminates the root problem or identifies the most appropriate opportunity for action. This is a long way from guessing at actions and haphazardly implementing them.

The tools include problem solving, planning, and project management. Implementing policy also involves a process for reviewing progress relative to plans.

Chapter 5. Implementing a Management-by-Policy System
Management by policy, as practiced by companies that have won the Deming Prize, represents the most advanced stage of TQ implementation. Chapter 5 describes how to implement such a system. It discusses prerequisites and success factors. This chapter explains how to benefit from all stages of MBP implementation, from novice to world class.

Chapter 6. The Spirit of Management by Policy
Executing management by policy to a world-class degree requires more than following procedures to the letter. It requires an extremely caring, sensitive approach. We conclude with a discussion of how to give management by policy the energy it needs to ensure breakthrough achievements.

Acknowledgments

The authors are indebted to a number of people for their help with this book:

Southern Pacific Lines and W. K. Sterett who encouraged us to organize our many ideas on management by policy in one place.

To Sandy Collins, Edward Conroy J.D., Clayton Fitzhugh, Steve Rust and Will Cogswell, who challenged our ideas and the presentation of them.

To Deltapoint for administrative support and its knowledge of the management by policy system. Colin Fox and Thom McDade, the founders of Deltapoint, were the first two persons in the United States to understand management by policy as practiced by the leading Japanese companies. Special mention goes to Craig Buxton, Chris Fosse, and Dr. Mike Rowney, who reviewed the manuscript and made superb contributions.

As part of its executive education process, Deltapoint has conducted over fifty Japanese Study Missions of Deming Prize winning companies. Consequently, Deltapoint has been able to understand the management systems that these outstanding companies have developed and are continually perfecting.

1

Total Quality—The Context of Management by Policy

If quality improvement could be reduced to one thought, it would be to reduce variation.

—Dr. W. Edwards Deming

The purpose of this chapter is to establish a common understanding of the principles of total quality (TQ) which represent the context of MBP. Implementing MBP should be considered only in this context.

A discussion of TQ must start with a definition of quality. Quality is meeting or exceeding customers' perceived needs. Excellent quality is meeting or exceeding needs to a degree that customers are enthusiastic about a company's products or services and will talk about them with other people.

In other words, customers' perceptions define quality. Nothing or no one else does. *Perception* is an important word because all that really counts is customers' perceptions relative to their expectations. For example, if a service is extremely reliable, but customers don't believe that it meets their reliability expectations, then quality is not good.

This definition also implies that companies must be sensitive to the process of creating and managing customer expectations. For example, care must be taken never to promise what can't be delivered. Even if quality has improved and is better than what the competition offers, making promises that cannot be fulfilled will lead to customer dissatisfaction.

Figure 1.1 is a model for putting these notions together. This model is an adaptation of the conceptual model of service quality presented by Zeithaml, Parasuraman, and Berry in *Delivering Quality Service*. Quality is determined by the gap between what is expected and what is perceived.

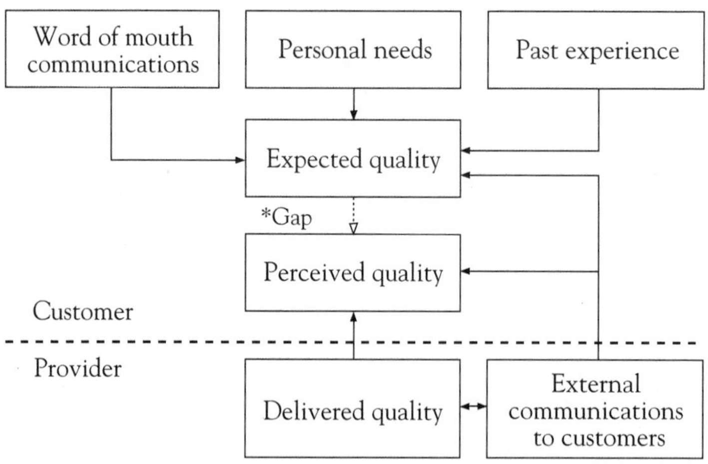

Figure 1.1: Conceptual model of service quality.

Because quality relates to all customer needs, there are many different categories of quality. Major categories of *product* quality include the following:

- Performance
- Features
- Serviceability/maintainability
- Reliability
- Durability
- Enhancibility
- Safety
- Environmental compatibility
- Compatibility with other products
- Transportability
- Ergometrics
- Aesthetics
- Price
- Delivery

Major categories of *service* quality include the following:

- Reliability
- Responsiveness
- Tangibles (appearance of facilities, equipment, and personnel)
- Competence
- Courtesy
- Credibility
- Security
- Accessibility
- Communication
- Understanding the customer

Quality also relates to customer satisfaction throughout the life of the product. It depends upon the degree to which the company is operating with corporate integrity and concern for the community.

Referring again to the definition of quality, customers are both external and internal to the organization. External customers for some products include distributors and retailers as well as the end users. Internal customers are employees of the company who receive the products or services of other employees. For example, a production operator on the shop floor is the customer of many departments—design engineering for product designs, material control for purchased parts used in production, and production control for schedules, to name only a few. In fact, virtually every person in every organization is simultaneously a customer and a supplier of at least one person and usually many more.

Why is it important to view employees as suppliers and customers? Paraphrasing Jan Carlzon, CEO of SAS, internal customers must be satisfied if the external customers are to be satisfied. If an airline ticket agent's needs for timely and reliable information aren't satisfied, then there's no way for the agent to satisfy the external customers' needs.

If quality is meeting or exceeding customers' perceived needs, then *total quality (TQ) is an organizational leadership and management philosophy which ensures that customers' perceived needs are continually being satisfied.* Although TQ was born of a need for businesses to be competitive globally, it is applicable to all organizations—domestic and local, churches, academia, public agencies, the armed services, health-care institutions, grocery stores, and so on. All organizations must anticipate their customers' needs and continuously improve products and services to meet ever-changing customer expectations.

Principles of TQ

Principle #1. Proactively and systematically understand current and future external and internal customer needs.

While customer complaint analysis is critical, it can only be done after the fact. *Proactively* means companies must anticipate customers' needs. To do so, companies must proactively assess customer needs. *Systematically* means that the process used to do this (for example, interviews, focus groups, and surveys) must be

- Valid (that is, ask the right questions in the right way).
- Objective, which in some situations requires third-party involvement in the assessment effort.
- Statistically reliable, which means consistent over time. To ensure this, surveys must be conducted periodically—ideally on a continuous basis.

Understanding customer needs is usually more difficult than it initially appears to be. When queried about products and services, customers often aren't sure about the reasons for their feelings and reactions. They can be vague when expressing their complaints or perceived needs. Consequently, survey results can be very misleading. Companies that do a good job of assessing customer needs spend enough time with customers to understand how they use the product or service. By interacting personally with customers as they use products or services, companies can understand customers' desires and thus the basis of their perceptions.

Interviewers must ask questions and not give answers. When customers express a need, ask for specific examples. Keep asking what customers mean until you get at least three levels of definition. Furthermore, it is critical to correlate all customer feedback, proactive and reactive, in order to validate conclusions about customer needs.

Principle #2. Proactively and systematically measure the customer's perception of how well your organization and your direct competitors satisfy these needs.

To cite Robert Galvin, former chairman and CEO of Motorola, "Only by measuring something can it be truly known." In order to be useful, customer satisfaction measurements must be both objective and reliable.

To ensure objectivity, a number of companies use a third party to assess customer satisfaction. Care must also be exercised that surveys and questionnaires don't bias the responses by the way questions are asked.

Reliable means that for any situation the measurement process will yield the same, or nearly the same, result. There must be a measurement process that is followed consistently. As Dr. Deming emphasizes, a measurement without a process isn't a valid measurement.

As important as the measurement itself is the analysis of the data. A number of companies assess customer satisfaction once a year and even base rewards on the change from year to year. Such analysis can yield erroneous conclusions. For example, one company obtained the following data when it measured responsiveness.

Year	Customers Who Feel Responsiveness Is Acceptable
1992	90%
1991	92%
Change from previous year	– 2%

This company concluded that responsiveness had deteriorated. In reality, responsiveness might or might not have worsened; there simply weren't enough data to obtain a statistically valid conclusion.

To ensure statistical validity, Boise Cascade randomly samples one-twelfth of its customers every month. In this way sufficient data can be obtained to assess whether variation in the data reflects a trend or just random variation. Measurements should be reported in statistical control chart format to ensure correct interpretation, as shown in Figure 1.2.

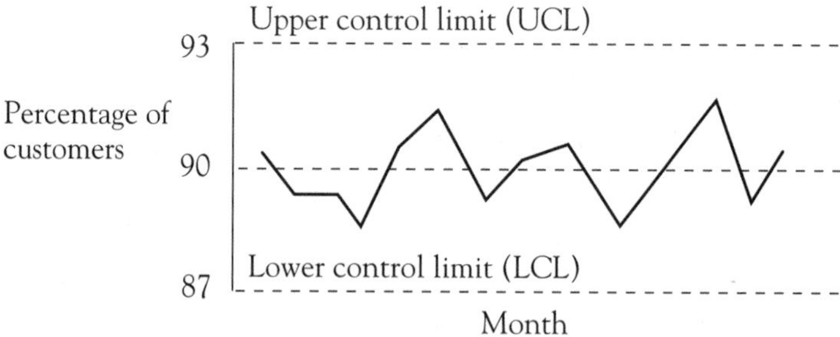

Figure 1.2: Percentage of customers who feel that responsiveness is acceptable.

Figure 1.2 shows that there is no real change in the percentage of customers who feel that responsiveness is acceptable. In order to conclude that there has been a change, the data must be either outside the control limits or otherwise indicate a trend (for example, there must be seven successively ascending data points).

Principle #3. Focus efforts on improving the processes or methods that satisfy customer needs. Better financial results such as cost reduction and higher profits are the outcome of process improvements.

This is a radical change from the traditional approach, which focuses only on financial results. Traditionally, in order to reduce costs, management set a cost-reduction objective and then identified the major categories of cost, such as work force. Invariably work force reductions were mandated. Unfortunately, customer service usually suffered.

The TQ approach would be to improve the process by streamlining it, reducing errors, shortening process cycle time, and eliminating activities that don't affect customer satisfaction. As a result, work force needs are decreased but customer satisfaction is enhanced—not worsened.

By focusing on the process first, there will be concurrent improvement in customer satisfaction and productivity. Improving quality improves productivity.

When the focus is on productivity, customer satisfaction almost always suffers. Increased customer satisfaction increases sales so that productivity gains can be realized without work-force reductions.

Principle #4. To improve quality, reduce process variation.

Variation is present in all activities and processes. Although they might be made or delivered according to the same design, there will be differences in parts, products, and services. In many instances, variation is within an acceptable tolerance band. For example, if the fat content of 1 percent skim milk is within 0.9 and 1.1 percent, it is acceptable according to the FDA. The variation, however, often exceeds acceptable limits, as Figure 1.3 shows.

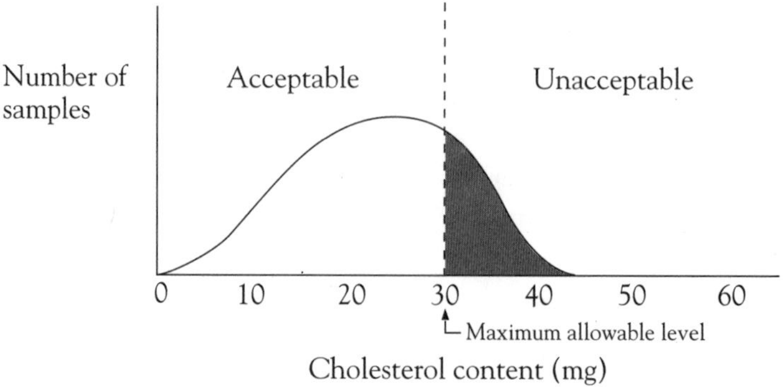

Figure 1.3: Distribution of cholesterol content of packaged food.

Sometimes even when the variation is within an acceptable design tolerance it is still not acceptable. In other words, zero defects (that is, everything is within specifications) isn't good enough. Sound contradictory? Ford Motor Company, which has made significant progress with its war on variation, uses an example that illustrates this point.

The same transmission was made within specifications by both Ford's Batavia, Ohio plant and by Mazda, in which Ford held about 20 percent ownership. Both transmissions were used by the same Ford assembly plant. After cars using Ford and Mazda transmissions had been in service for some time, Ford started receiving customer complaints about rough-shifting transmissions.

Analysis revealed that all the complaints were about the Ford-made transmissions. Further analysis of those transmissions showed that, although the Ford part dimensions all met specifications, there was greater variation *within those specifications* than there was with the Mazda parts. Customers noticed the increased shifting roughness resulting from this variation.

Process capability refers to the comparison of the requirement for a given quality characteristic to the inherent range of process variation for that characteristic. For example, if the requirements for a dimension can vary between 6.745 cm and 6.755 cm and the inherent variability is 0.005 cm, the process capability is

$$\frac{\text{Requirements}}{\text{Process variation}} = \frac{6.755 - 6.745 \text{ cm}}{0.005 \text{ cm}} = \frac{0.010}{0.005} = 2.0$$

Using this formula to determine process capability makes one critical assumption: that the process is centered or located at or near the target value. In this example, although the dimensional requirements can vary between 6.745 cm and 6.755 cm, the target value is 6.750 cm (see Figure 1.4a).

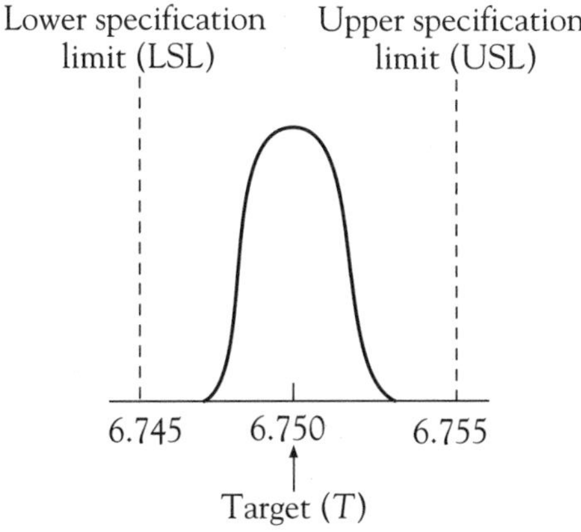

Figure 1.4a: The process is centered at the target value of 6.750 cm.

Figure 1.4b shows, if the process were centered on 6.745, it would not be capable because 50 percent of the time it would be outside of the lower specification limit. Therefore, in order for a process to be *capable, it must be properly centered or located and the process variation must be less than the allowable range of requirements.* To consider both location and variation, a process capability index ratio C_{pk} is used.

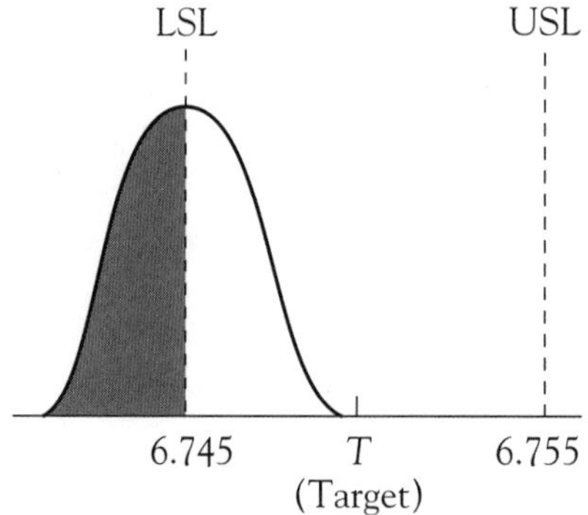

Figure 1.4b: The same process is not capable if it is centered at 6.745 cm.

$$C_{pk} = \left|\frac{\bar{X} - LSL}{3\sigma}\right| \text{ or } \left|\frac{USL - \bar{X}}{3\sigma}\right|, \text{ whichever is less}$$

Where $\bar{X}$ is the process average, that is, where the process is centered and 3σ = one-half of the process variation.

If the process in our example were centered on 6.745, then C_{pk} would be 0.

$$C_{pk} = \left|\frac{\bar{X} - LSL}{3\sigma}\right| \text{ or } \left|\frac{USL - \bar{X}}{3\sigma}\right|, \text{ whichever is less}$$

$$= \frac{6.745 - 6.745}{\frac{1}{2}(.005)} \text{ or } \frac{6.755 - 6.745}{\frac{1}{2}(.005)}$$

$$0 \text{ or } 2$$

In the Ford-Mazda example the process capability for various quality characteristics was significantly greater for the Mazda transmissions than for the Ford transmissions, as shown in Figure 1.4c.

Causes of Variation

Variation is due to either common or special causes. The nature of the variation determines the strategy for reducing it.

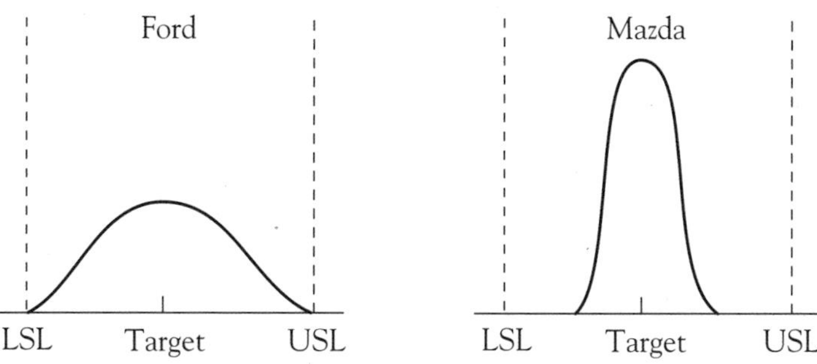

Figure 1.4c: Process capability comparison for a quality characteristic.

Common causes of process variation are ever present and vary randomly within some statistical distribution. Therefore, common cause or *random* variation is predictable. That is, one may predict that the variation will be somewhere within the statistical distribution most of the time. *Inherent* or common cause variation from point to point cannot be explained because the variation is due only to the process and is ever present. Problems due to common causes are also said to be chronic because they exist continually.

Special causes of variation are those outside the common causes that are ever present. The variation is due to specific assignable causes that are nonrandom occurrences. Special causes are sporadic and not predictable.

Consider a commuter whose drive to work varies between 30 and 50 minutes, even though she uses the same route and leaves at about the same time every day. The 20-minute range in time results from the inherent or common causes of variation in the process of driving to work.

- Starting time
- Traffic density
- Weather
- Driving styles of other motorists

One day there was a serious accident on the route, so it took the commuter 90 minutes to get to work. The accident was a nonrandom event or a special cause of the variation that led to the usual 30- to 50-minute process being exceeded. As with most special causes, this one was eliminated fairly quickly by removing the wreckage from the street.

To consistently keep her commute under 30 minutes, the commuter needed to make fundamental changes in the process. In this case, she did so by creating a two-person car pool. By carpooling, she was able to use the high occupancy vehicle lane (a lane specially designated for cars with two or more persons), which had less traffic. Then the trip took between 15 and 20 minutes. The average time and variation were significantly reduced.

In the previous example of process capability, the inherent capability due to common, ever-present causes of variation was 0.005, varying from 6.7475 and 6.7525 when centered on target. One day a new person, who had insufficient training, was assigned to the operation. As a result, the machined dimension varied from 6.700 to 6.850, which was outside of what the system normally produced. This excessive variation was due to an assignable cause, that is, the lack of knowledge, correctable by appropriate training (see Figure 1.5).

A control chart is used to identify whether variation is due to common or special causes. Control limits are established for the process such that 99.97 percent of the time a process that is in control (that is, when only common causes are present), will produce a dimension that falls within these limits. If a dimension falls outside these limits or if the pattern within the limits does not appear to be random (for example, seven dimensions above or below the average), then there is evidence of a special cause. In other words, if variation is due only to common causes the probability of a point falling outside the control limits is so low that one can conclude that the variation is due to a special cause.

It is important to know whether or not variation is due only to special or common causes because the strategy for dealing with each differs.

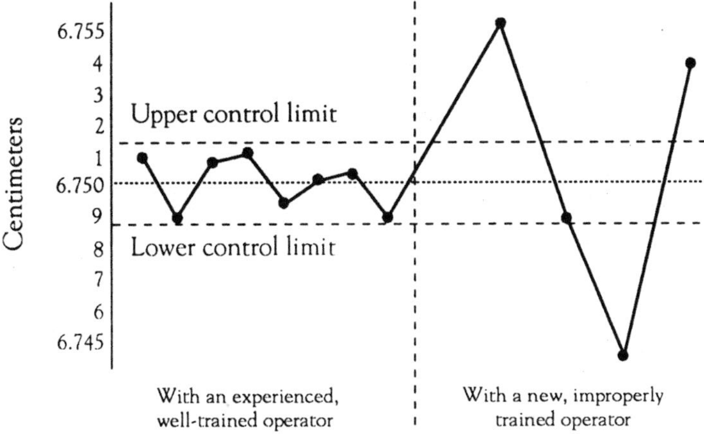

Figure 1.5: Differences in variation within the control limits between an experienced operator and an untrained operator.

This is a critical point. With special causes the process should be stopped immediately and the special causes identified and corrected. Usually this can be done by the persons who are operating within the system.

If only common causes are present the system is said to be stable or in control. The first analytical step is to determine the system's process capability. If the process isn't capable then, in order to reduce variation, the process must be changed. Changing the process takes longer, usually requires more effort and investment, and, therefore, needs management's attention.

Understanding the nature of variation has profound implications. Instead of first asking what or who caused the variation, one should first ask what is the nature of the variation. If the variation is due to a common cause, then it is a waste of time to try to explain the reasons for point-to-point variation.

Think of all of the time that can be spent trying to explain undesirable common-cause variations, such as the percent of scheduled deliveries that weren't met on time. Most of this time is wasted.

One of the greatest maladies of industrial life is that management treats almost all variation as if it were due to special causes. Frequently management takes action when it should leave the process alone. Management's actions usually make things a lot worse, not better. In other words, *overadjustment increases variation*.

The supervisor of an insurance company's claim-processing department was about to fire an employee for having an error rate of 12 per month, which was above the group's average of 7 per month. But, when the capability of the entire department was determined relative to the errors made, the employee's errors were found to be within the system. That is, the individual's error rate was within expected variation in error rate due to common causes (0 to 14 errors). Therefore, there was no statistical evidence to support the supervisor's contention that the employee was making an excessive percentage of errors. Figure 1.6 shows a control chart for this claims department.

Genichi Taguchi, four-time winner of the Deming Prize for individual contribution, brought attention to variation by quantifying the loss or dissatisfaction due to variation by what he calls a loss function (see Figure 1.7). Taguchi believes that for many situations in nature where the nominal or target value is best, the loss varies from the target value according to the following relationship.

$$L(\$) = K\,(x - t)^2 \qquad K = \text{constant},\ T = \text{target}$$

Taguchi's loss function makes intuitive sense. For example, actual room temperature can vary a few degrees above or below the target temperature without any effect on the people in the room. At some point, however, variation from target will cause significant discomfort. Consequently, the old tenet of zero defects has been replaced by the new tenet of zero variation.

Principle #5. Develop robust designs for products and processes. The old approach to product design was for engineers to assume that they knew what the customers wanted, to produce a design, and then to make corrections to it based on feedback from internal and external customers. The new approach is to proactively assess

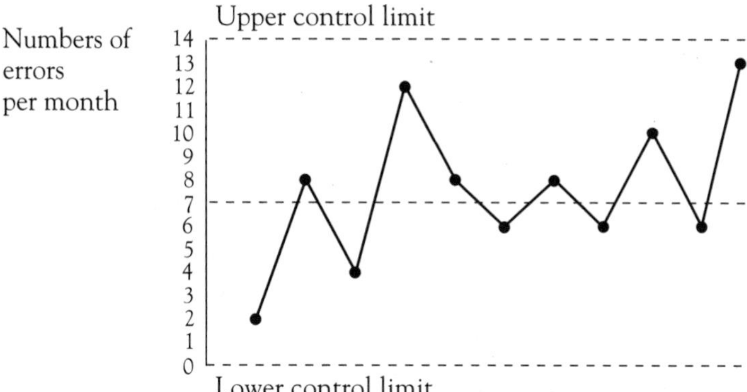

Figure 1.6: Control chart for insurance claims errors. Note that the number of errors per month for the employee in question (that is, 12) is within the upper and lower control limits.

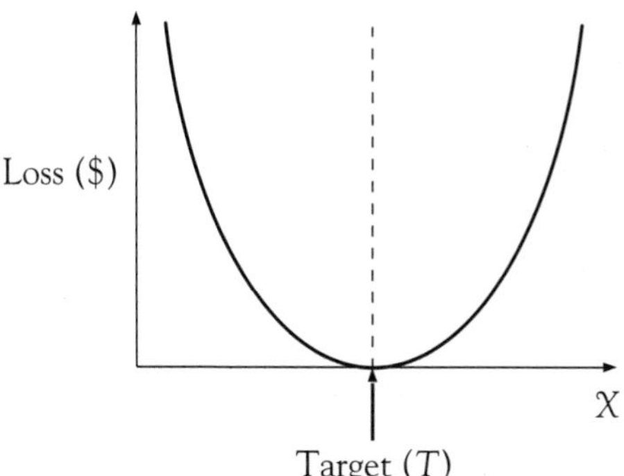

Figure 1.7: Taguchi's loss function.

customer needs and then to concurrently design products and processes with production, purchasing, and suppliers. Product designers aim for a *robust design*.

Robust designs are not sensitive to variations of production processes, components, raw materials, and customer usage. The traditional engineering approach designs to a target (target value, target function, target region), then reduces variation around the target. The new approach, developed by Genichi Taguchi, is to design for robust function, then adjust to target.

Traditional designers tighten tolerances and use higher-grade materials to improve product performance and reliability. With the new approach, engineers achieve the best possible performance and reliability with low-cost material first, and upgrade only as a last resort. Consequently, the Taguchi approach results in the best performance at lowest cost.

Development of robust design requires extensive use of statistically designed experiments and testing. Although developed by Sir Ronald Fisher in the 1910s, experimental design is still seldom included in the curricula of engineering schools today.

Many U.S. companies have initiated quality improvement efforts mainly in manufacturing. There is considerably more leverage for improvement in the product and process engineering area. Although engineering accounts for about 5 percent of the budget, it affects 70 to 80 percent of the improvement opportunity.

TQ must be implemented in every area of the business. However, if there were only one place to start in a manufacturing company, we would recommend exposing engineers to the new methods of robust design.

The Japanese have developed an excellent process to organize and facilitate product and process design. They call it quality function deployment (QFD). QFD is a process for translating customer needs into product technical requirements or design specifications. These specifications are, in turn, translated into system, subsystem, and component requirements.

For each component a process is established and a process control plan developed. Using a series of interrelated matrices, the customer requirements are ultimately linked to process control plans and parameters. Competitive comparisons are integrated into the QFD structure to identify significant competitive differences. In this way, QFD shows where to focus product and process development efforts for competitive advantage.

Principle #6. Use the scientific method for solving problems and improving processes.

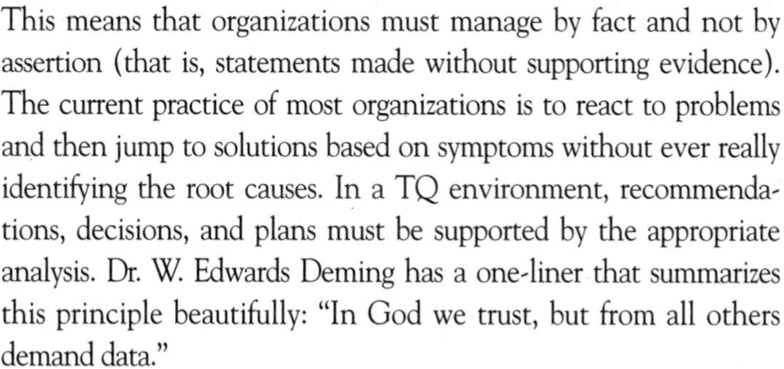

This means that organizations must manage by fact and not by assertion (that is, statements made without supporting evidence). The current practice of most organizations is to react to problems and then jump to solutions based on symptoms without ever really identifying the root causes. In a TQ environment, recommendations, decisions, and plans must be supported by the appropriate analysis. Dr. W. Edwards Deming has a one-liner that summarizes this principle beautifully: "In God we trust, but from all others demand data."

Managing by fact really means applying the scientific process, which is described very succinctly by the plan-do-check-act (PDCA) cycle (see Figure 1.8). This graphical representation of the scientific method was developed in the twenties by Walter A. Shewhart, then of AT&T's famous Hawthorne plant. The Japanese call PDCA the Deming cycle. Deming calls it the Shewhart cycle.

(Dr. Deming worked in R&D at Hawthorne when Dr. Shewhart was there, but the two didn't work together until several years later in New York and Washington. Coincidentally, Dr. Joseph M. Juran worked there in inspection and knew Shewhart.)

The scientific method is applied by starting at the plan step of the PDCA cycle and going clockwise around the wheel. Quality improvement is a never-ending cycle of turning this wheel, so to speak, on business processes. A total quality management system is a structured process that concurrently turns the wheel on

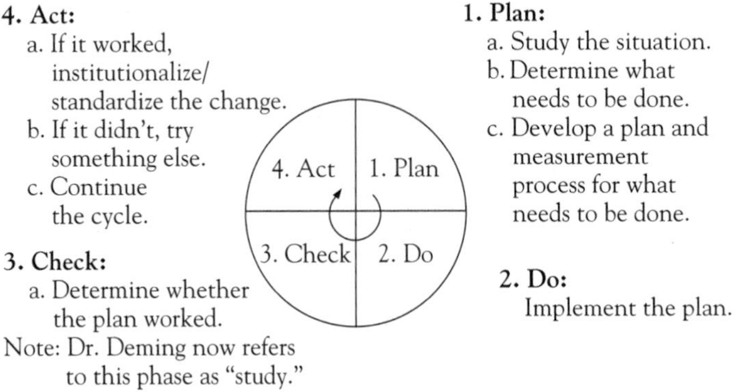

4. Act:
a. If it worked, institutionalize/ standardize the change.
b. If it didn't, try something else.
c. Continue the cycle.
3. Check:
a. Determine whether the plan worked.
Note: Dr. Deming now refers to this phase as "study."
4. Act
1. Plan
3. Check
2. Do
1. Plan:
a. Study the situation.
b. Determine what needs to be done.
c. Develop a plan and measurement process for what needs to be done.
2. Do:
Implement the plan.

Figure 1.8: The plan-do-check-act (PDCA) cycle.

business processes to improve their standards while conducting business at the current standard.

American managers typically spend most of their time in the do step, reacting to problems and treating the symptoms instead of the root causes. Very little effort is made to identify root causes. The ace firefighter or hero who saves the day, albeit temporarily, is richly rewarded. By comparison, the more reflective, analytical employee, who takes time to understand what is happening is often viewed as indecisive and unassertive.

If good analysis is rare, then determining whether the corrective action worked and verifying that it did by quantitative measurements is even rarer, and the act step almost nonexistent. That is, when the effectiveness of a countermeasure is verified, it is usually not institutionalized by standardization throughout the organization. Consequently, there will be backsliding, and gains from improvement will be lost.

The plan step includes the following substeps.

1. Identify the customer.
2. Understand the customer's expectations.

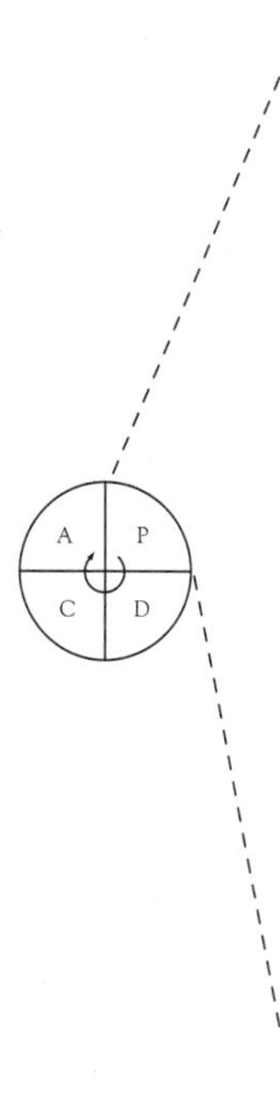

3. Measure customer satisfaction. Identify and prioritize gaps between the customer's perceptions and expectations.
4. Understand the process that provides the product or service.
   - Make a flowchart of the process.
   - Identify the root causes of gaps.
   - Determine whether the process is stable (in statistical control) or unstable.
5. If the process is unstable, stabilize it or design it to be more robust (that is, insensitive to variation).
6. If the process is stable, determine if it is capable.
7. If the process is capable, determine the appropriate process control plan.
8. If the process is not capable, then study alternatives to improve the process.
9. Select an alternative or countermeasure.
10. Develop a plan to implement the alternatives and develop measurements to determine the effect of the plan.

Substep 4 utilizes the following seven basic improvement tools.

1. Flowchart
2. Cause-and-effect diagram
3. Pareto chart
4. Scatter diagram
5. Histogram
6. Run chart
7. Control chart

For a description of these tools refer to Appendix A.

For companies that are relatively new to using the quality improvement process (those in the first several years of implementation), using flowcharts, cause-and-effect diagrams, and Pareto charts alone can provide significant benefits.

A variation of the PDCA cycle is called the standardize-do-check-act (SDCA) cycle. The standardize step is used to plan for the replication of a given process that is standard throughout the organization. The do step implements the standardization plan. The check step determines whether any backsliding has occurred.

In addition to the seven basic tools, which have been used collectively since the 1960s (some individual tools much longer), there are seven other tools. These are the management or new planning tools. They were identified by a research effort of the Japanese Union of Scientists and Engineers (JUSE), the results of which were published in 1977. Since then their application has continued to grow; they are now used extensively in Japan by companies committed to TQ. For a description of these planning tools refer to Appendix B.

The new tools are powerful. In analysis they help to identify the most significant root causes. Once a root cause and its solution are identified, some of the tools are used to develop a plan with the maximum probability for success.

Principle #7. When there are problems, or expectations haven't been met, look to the system. Don't blame people.

This principle follows from the proposition that at least 85 percent of all variation is due to the system. The system is the responsibility of management, not of the person or persons who are working within it.

Usually, when there is unfavorable variation of any kind (such as missed schedules, rejects, equipment downtime, or loss of a customer), management's first impulse is usually to blame an individual or group of individuals; however, only 15 percent or less of the time is the problem caused by people. Instead, variation is usually due to bad material or bad information used during the process, the method, the measurement process, the environment, or the machine. Even if the problem is due to a person, frequently the root cause of the problem is with management. Lack of proper training is a widespread example of this.

Instead of finger pointing, management should focus on the system. Instead of asking "Who did it?" or "Who didn't do it?" management should ask "What is wrong with the system?"

Paradoxically, because the whole system is controlled by management and not by people who work inside the system, management should be pointing its finger at itself, if at anyone. This is another classic example of Pogo's "We have met the enemy and they are us."

Commitment to Principle #7 is critical to making significant and lasting improvement. If management demonstrates a commitment to this principle, people will willingly identify problems and areas of opportunity. If management is not committed, most people will keep quiet, do only what they are told, and would fear management retribution if they were to make suggestions for improvement.

Principle #8. Emphasize prevention instead of detection.
The old way of ensuring quality is to have someone do something and then have someone else inspect it. Not only does this not work (studies have shown that inspection is only 80 percent effective), but it costs a lot of money.

Inspection does not add value and it doesn't improve quality. It only helps ensure that what goes to the customers is okay. When people know that someone else is going to check their work, they don't feel accountable and are less careful, thinking that the subsequent inspection process will catch any problems.

The new way empowers and trains people to be their own inspectors. They inspect what they do while they're doing it, ideally at no additional cost. Critical process control parameters (also called checkpoints) are identified and controlled so that output of the process (also called control points) won't need to be inspected.

For example, a specialty chemicals company knows that if time, acidity, temperature, and pressure are maintained at target levels within narrow bands around these values, the output of the process will be optimized. The ultimate way to ensure quality, however, is to design processes so that regardless of variation of process control parameters, the output is optimal or nearly optimal. Such processes are said to be robust designs. A related concept is the notion of fail safing, or *poka-yoke* in Japanese. To fail safe a process means to design it so that it can't go wrong, or, if that isn't possible, to automatically stop the process when something does go wrong.

For example, consider Setex, which supplies car seats to Honda U.S.A. Setex has designed a jig that won't release the seat frame until bolts are torqued down to the right specifications. In Setex's robotic welding area, if parts are loaded incorrectly on the welding jig, the robot won't function. There is a spectrum of approaches to ensure quality, ranging from bad to outstanding.

Bad ◄--------------	Good -----------►	Outstanding
Inspection after the fact	Process parameter control	Robust process design
		Fail safing (*poka-yoke*)

Principle #9. Put quality ahead of quantity.

In many businesses quality standards are relaxed at the end of the month in order to achieve monthly output goals. For example, in a major insurance company, customers complained about the long claim-processing times. Management's knee-jerk response was to mandate a reduction in backlog to reduce the processing time. The claims-processing department responded by shortcutting the process. Claims-processing errors rose dramatically, which increased customer complaints and actually increased the variation and the average claim-processing time. In another example, a Fortune 500 company arbitrarily cut the time to close the books at month's end from ten to four days. As a result, accuracy decreased.

Putting quality ahead of quantity means

1. Consistent quality standards
2. Never passing on known or suspected bad quality to the next person in the process (the internal customer)
3. Reward systems, nonfinancial as well as financial, that give priority to quality and process improvement
4. Allocating sufficient resources to work on improvement

Principle #10. Benchmark against the direct competition and against the best in the world, regardless of whether they are direct competitors. Standardize the best-known practices. Although it is important for an organization to compare itself against its direct competitors, it is more important for it to compare itself against the best in the world and to learn from the best to make its processes even better. For a time U.S. automakers compared themselves only against companies they considered direct competitors—other U.S. companies. Unfortunately, new competitors from Japan that had developed better methods entered the U.S. market. In the future, chances are that companies will face increasing numbers of competitors that don't exist today.

The best way to ensure sustained competitive superiority is to continually compare your company's processes with how the best perform the same processes. That doesn't mean that the best process should be duplicated, but it should at least be studied so the company can use whichever aspects will improve its own process. A company might have the best overall process, but it isn't necessarily doing every part of the process better than anyone else. A World Series championship baseball team, for example, has the best overall team process, but isn't necessarily best at every position.

Table 1.1 is a representative sample of critical business processes and the companies considered by many to have some of the best processes in the world.

Standardization, having all persons follow the current best practice, is a major opportunity for many North American firms. Standardization to the degree that the great Japanese companies do

Critical business procedure	Companies with a world-class process
▪ Benchmarking process	Xerox
▪ Customer contact	SAS
▪ Customer needs assessment	GTE
▪ Customer relationships	IBM (Rochester, Minnesota)
▪ Education	Motorola
▪ Employee recognition process	Milliken
▪ Internal communication	Federal Express
▪ Leadership involvement and education	Milliken
▪ New employee selection	Toyota, Honda, Nissan
▪ New product design and development	Toyota, Honda, Sony
▪ Order processing	L. L. Bean
▪ Management by policy	Toyota, Canon, Florida Power and Light
▪ Supplier management	Motorola, Xerox
▪ Transaction processing	American Express
▪ Quality information system (repository of process improvement learnings)	Credit Card Services Toyota, Aisen Seiki

Table 1.1: Companies with commonly benchmarked processes.

will require a cultural breakthrough at many companies. Regrettably, standardization seems to have a negative connotation for many people for several reasons.

1. The mistaken perception that standardization inhibits creativity. Actually, standardization facilitates creativity by eliminating abnormalities and, thereby, allows attention to be focused on real improvement. Standards must be continually revised to reflect continuous improvement of practices. According to Ishikawa, "When standards are not being revised, technical progress has halted."
2. Standards are synonymous with bureaucratic procedures, which are inhibiting.

Irrespective of the negative connotation, standardization must become a widespread practice in all departments and at all organization levels. Without it, gains will only be partially realized and will erode over time. Management's job is to train people to observe the standards and to ensure that they do so. The key to effective standardization is to involve persons who will need to observe a standard in the development of that standard. Although not as glamorous as improvement, standardization offers tremendous payback opportunities.

Principle #11. Develop long-term relationships with suppliers committed to TQ.

Traditionally, purchasing agents have played suppliers against each other to secure the lowest initial cost. Superior quality has rarely been in the purchasing equation—it's been a distant second priority at best. World-class companies realize that

1. Their suppliers must also be world-class TQ companies.
2. Their suppliers must be intimately involved in the company's planning and design process.

3. They must secure suppliers with the lowest total cost, not lowest initial cost. This means having suppliers with the best quality, because bad quality costs more. In traditional companies the price of nonconformance (PON) which, simply put, is the price of not doing things right the first time, ranges from 20 to 40 percent of sales! PON consists of the following:
   - External failures—the cost of fixing a bad product or service in the field. Includes such things as warranty expense.
   - Internal failures—the cost of failures before they leave the company. This includes rework, scrap, machine downtime, safety disruptions, and extra in-process inventory as a contingency for these problems.
   - Appraisal—the cost of finding failures before bad products or services leave the company.

In world-class companies, PON ranges from three to five percent of sales, which is why these companies have a significant cost advantage over their traditional competitors.

One implication of this new thinking about suppliers is that companies can afford only to have one supplier for a given product or service for several reasons. Given the intimate relationships required, having more than one means that there is now more than one source of variation, which complicates the process of reducing variation.

This type of thinking represents a new paradigm. Having such a relationship requires a very high degree of trust and commitment between the customer and the supplier. This degree of trust usually develops over a long period of time as both companies take small steps until they can take the great leap toward having one customer/supplier. Developing trust requires openness about costs and capabilities.

Principle #12. Empower all employees in the improvement process.

World-class quality requires that every individual has three concurrent jobs!

Job #1 Maintaining and performing the job at the current job standard.

Job #2 Improving the way the job is performed (improving the job standard).

Job #3 Participating in the planning process, which enables everyone to do all three jobs.

Clearly, the amount of time spent in each of these endeavors will vary greatly depending on each person's role in the company. Typically, nonmanagement personnel will spend much less time with jobs #2 and #3 than will management.

Figure 1.9 shows the approximate percentages of time spent by various organizational levels from the top floor to the first line. Note that at the lowest level of the organization (the first line) approximately ten percent of the time is spent in improvement and planning. This new expectation clearly demonstrates what behavioral scientists have been recommending for years—to ensure commitment to change, involve those persons who will have to live with the change in its design, planning, and implementation.

In addition to this new expectation of involvement in planning, maintaining, and improving the current standard, the meaning of involvement has two other components.

1. People are expected to use their discretion, and, when they feel it appropriate, exceed the service standard to satisfy customers.
2. When they see evidence of special or assignable causes disrupting a process, they are authorized to stop the process.

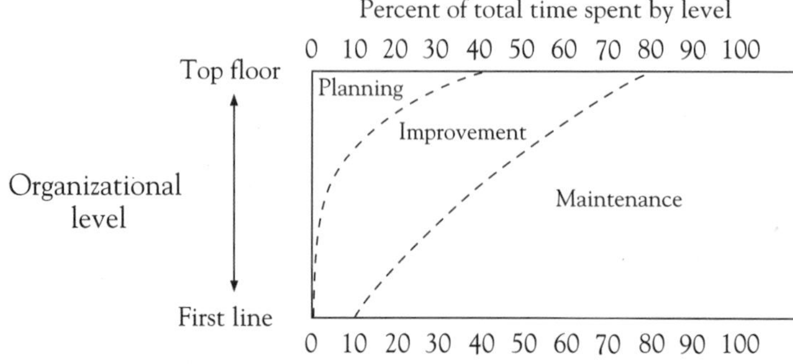

Adapted from Masaaki Imai, Kaizen, *1986.*

Figure 1.9: Typical percentage of time spent at different organizational levels on planning, improvement, and maintenance.

Principle #13. Develop the capability of people to their fullest potential.

This principle is at the heart of total quality. Improving the capability of people is a prerequisite to improving the capability of processes and systems, which in turn is a prerequisite to improving products and services. Sony chairman Akio Morita's definition of the ultimate competitive advantage captures the essence of this element. To paraphrase Morita, the ultimate competitive advantage is utilizing the creative energies of all Sony employees to a greater degree than its competition utilizes the creative energies of its employees. The key value is to treat people as assets whose value appreciates over time.

All companies have access to essentially the same resources—people, information, capital, and technology. The half-life of engineers is estimated to be no more than seven years. What makes a lasting difference? It is the environment of the company and the degree to which people are developed.

Leadership development is the foundation for implementing a TQ system. Developing people, involving them to the degree we've discussed, and empowering them requires the following significant changes in the traditional leadership model.

From	To
Commander, boss ("Do what you're told")	Coach, facilitator, teacher, mentor
Controller ("People need to be controlled.")	Leader—by shared purpose, vision, values, and beliefs; commitment to the purpose and values provides control
Individualist	Team builder
Internally competitive	Internally cooperative, externally competitive
Withholding	Open, always explaining why
Owner mentality ("It's my company. You work for me. I pay your salary. Do what you're told to do.")	Trustee mentality ("I don't own the company; I've been entrusted with it and am responsible for providing an environment in which people can have a fulfilled life.")

Principle #14. View the organization as a network focused on customers.

The old way to view an organization is on a vertical hierarchy of functions—the military model based upon rank (see Figure 1.10a). The new way to view the organization is as a horizontal network of suppliers and customers that cuts across functions (see Figure 1.10b).

While bosses are depicted very prominently on the old vertical hierarchy, they are less obvious in the new model. In the new model the boss is also another customer and supplier, whose principal task is to enable people to satisfy their customers by improving processes that provide goods or services.

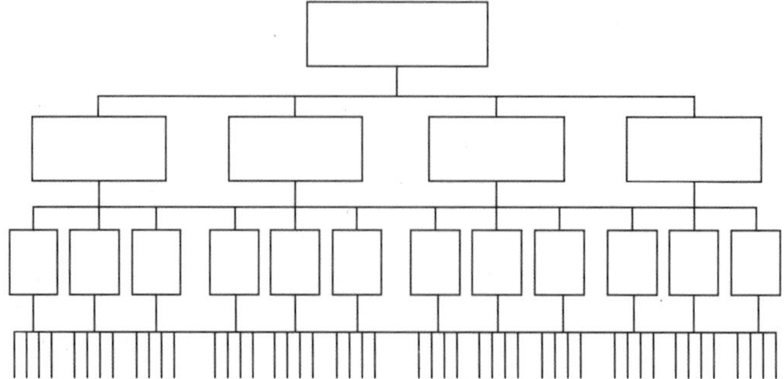

Figure 1.10a: In this organizational model, the most important person to any individual is the boss. As long as the boss is satisfied, security is usually intact.

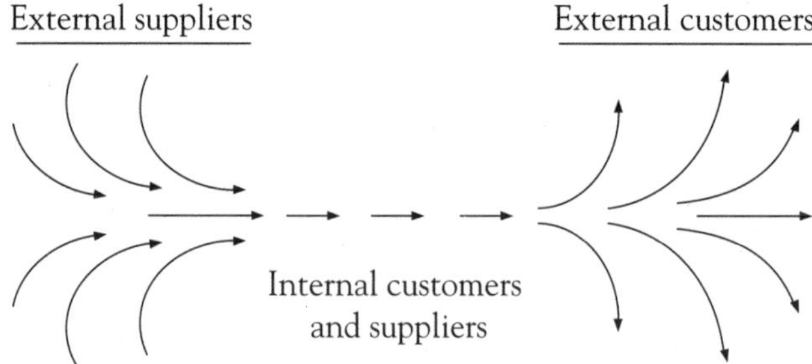

Adapted from W. E. Deming

Figure 1.10b: The new horizontally oriented view of an organization.

To emphasize the horizontal organization and the need for cross-functional management, excellent Japanese companies have created permanent committees for major categories of customer satisfaction (including quality, safety, delivery, cost, and morale/social responsibility), and for major processes, especially new product design and development. These committees comprise senior-level managers who represent major functional areas.

The purpose of these committees is to plan for and coordinate improvement efforts relative to their respective areas. Taken together, the structure and workings of these committees have been termed cross-functional management by the Japanese.

Principle #15. Reward people in ways that put quality improvement first.

The single biggest deterrent to total quality implementation is that the reward systems, financial as well as nonfinancial, are inconsistent with the quality improvement principles previously discussed. Financial compensation systems must reflect the following:

1. Individuals must not be held accountable for outcomes over which they have no control.
2. Accountability for cross-functional objectives should be shared by the functions involved. It is not possible to quantitatively determine the percentage contribution of each function for cross-functional objectives.
3. Do not force-rank individuals, because most persons operate within the system. If people are operating within the system, it is wrong to say that because one person had 0.2 percent defects compared to another person making 0.3 percent defects that the person with a lower defect rate was a better performer and, therefore, warrants more money.
4. Develop a process to provide feedback to individuals from internal and external suppliers and customers, including the boss. The spirit of the feedback process should be to help people improve, not to judge their performance.
5. Base compensation on the going market rate, increased capability, added responsibilities, experience, and overall business results.
6. Ensure that profit sharing is equitable.

Some people are clearly outside the system and perform extraordinarily well or badly. When this is the case, special treatment is appropriate, such as a bonus for the former and help for the latter.

Nonfinancial reward/recognition systems must be designed with great care. Every time an individual or team is recognized for something, other individuals or teams might feel overlooked. This can cause resentment if the recognition or lack of it is perceived as unequitable. Usually, companies are quick to recognize the success of improvement team efforts but don't realize that it was the people doing the day-to-day job who made it possible for the improvement team to work on its project. Recognizing the improvement team and not the others can cause problems.

The guiding principle must be: recognize individuals less and celebrate the entire organization's success more. Evolve from extrinsically based recognition processes (such as an article in the company newspaper about a specific team), to a more intrinsic orientation. This means that persons derive their satisfaction primarily from receiving feedback from customers, suppliers, and peers recognizing their competence. A simple thank-you seems to work best. The customer-supplier review process is a key vehicle for providing this feedback.

Principle #16. Focus on the significant few problems.

In most endeavors there is a persistent tendency to try to do too much. As a result, resources might be spread too thin and little, if anything, will be accomplished. Companies that develop self-discipline to identify and work on only the significant few problems will probably have an advantage over their competitors.

A major tenet of total quality is to apply the observation of a 19th century Italian economist, Vilfredo Pareto: "In any population, a relatively small percentage of items account for any attribute of the population." For example, a small percentage of the root causes of a problem accounts for most of the undesirable effects.

Applying this principle is fundamental to management by policy. In essence, management by policy is a process that identifies and aligns all resources of the business to accomplish two or three major improvement initiatives that will provide significant competitive advantage.

Summary

Principle #1 Proactively and systematically understand external and internal customer needs.

Principle #2 Proactively and systematically assess the customer's perception of how well your organization and your direct competitors satisfy these needs.

Principle #3 Focus efforts on improving the processes or methods that satisfy customer needs. Better financial results such as cost reduction and profits are the outcomes of process improvements.

Principle #4 To improve quality, reduce process variation.

Principle #5 Develop robust product and process designs.

Principle #6 Use the scientific method for solving problems and improving processes.

Principle #7 When there are problems, look to the system. Don't blame people.

Principle #8 Emphasize prevention instead of detection.

Principle #9 Always put quality ahead of quantity.

Principle #10 Benchmark against the direct competition and against the best in the world, regardless of whether they are direct competitors. Standardize the best-known practices.

Principle #11 Develop long-term relationships with suppliers committed to TQ.

Principle #12 Empower all employees in the improvement process.

Principle #13 Develop the capability of people to their fullest potential.

Principle #14 View the organization as a network focused on customers.

Principle #15 Reward people in ways that put quality improvement first.

Principle #16 Focus on the significant few problems.

2

Implementing Total Quality

TQC is not a fast-acting drug like penicillin but a slow activity herbal remedy that will gradually improve a company's constitution if taken over a long period.

—Dr. Kaoru Ishikawa

Since implementing total quality transforms the way the entire business is run, top management must lead the change process. In some large companies, TQ began successfully in either a division or in a functional area such as manufacturing. But unless top management becomes actively involved, leading the implementation throughout the entire company, the process ultimately grinds to a stop far short of world-class competency. Because change is so difficult and total quality entails such a huge change, top management must become impassioned with this effort. Total quality implementation must be their number-one priority!

There need not be a key position in the company, such as a corporate director or vice president of quality, for coordinating implementation efforts. If there is, however, this person's staff must be kept small, less than five, even in companies with annual revenues over $1 billion, to ensure that it has only a coordinating role and not an implementation role. Line management must be accountable for implementing total quality. It can't be delegated to a staff or a TQ program office. The journey to world-class competency can be described in terms of the following phases.

Phase 1	Leadership education, involvement, and planning
Phase 2	Companywide introduction
Phase 3	Implementation of a proactive, prevention-based approach on major business systems
Phase 4	Culture of continuous process improvement
Phase 5	World-class results

Phase 1. Leadership Education, Involvement, and Planning

Top management begins by understanding the principles of total quality and their implications and benefits. Then, visits to leading TQ companies and discussions with other top executives are usually very beneficial. Many executives have hurriedly visited Deming Award winners in Japan without adequate preparation. They came back disappointed and unimpressed. Unfortunately, they didn't know what questions to ask. As Deming might say, they did not know what they didn't know. The following is a suggested initial curriculum for general managers.

Course/Subject	Hours
1. Total quality overview	24
2. Leading cultural change	8
3. Statistical thinking for managers (Understanding and dealing with variation in their daily lives)	8

4. Understanding and using the Malcolm Baldrige National Quality Award criteria	12
5. Management by policy overview (How to plan and focus improvement efforts)	4
6. Overview of the new engineering paradigm	4
7. Management's role in TQ implementation	12
TOTAL	72

This "classroom" time must be supplemented by related readings. TQ is synonymous with the notion of a learning organization.

Milliken's top management is the epitome of a learning organization. Even after winning the Malcolm Baldrige National Quality Award, this company engaged a consulting firm to introduce them to the management systems of world-class Japanese companies. Top management preparation involved the equivalent of seven classroom days and the reading of 12 books. Each manager was required to present to other top managers a summary of the key concepts and the implications to Milliken from six of these books. The education process starts with top management, but it doesn't end there. Ultimately, the total management team must experience the same educational process.

When there is sufficient understanding of TQ principles and their implications, top management is prepared to first create a mission for the company or to reassess its current mission statement. A mission statement explains why the organization exists, what business the enterprise is in, and the scope of the business.

The next step is to create an operation philosophy or credo that describes how the enterprise will accomplish the mission given that TQ is the prevailing mind-set. It includes the values, beliefs, and principles by which an organization operates and is written in a way that touches both the hearts and the minds of all employees.

The following is an example of mission, values, and guiding philosophy statements—those of the Ford Motor Company.

Mission

Ford Motor Company is a worldwide leader in automotive and automotive-related products and services as well as in newer industries such as aerospace, communications, and financial services. Our mission is to continually improve our products and services to meet our customers' needs, allowing us to prosper as a business and to provide a reasonable return for our stockholders, the owners of our business.

Values

How we accomplish our mission is as important as the mission itself. Fundamental to success for the company are these basic values.

People

Our people are the source of our strength. They provide our corporate intelligence and determine our reputation and vitality. Involvement and teamwork are our core human values.

Products

Our products are the end result of our efforts, and they should be the best in serving customers worldwide. As our products are viewed, so are we viewed.

Profits

Profits are the ultimate measure of how efficiently we provide customers with the best products for their needs. Profits are required to survive and grow.

Guiding Principles

Quality comes first—to achieve customer satisfaction, the quality of our products and services must be our number-one priority.

Customers are the focus of everything we do—our work must be done with our customers in mind, providing better products and services than our competition.

> Continuous improvement is essential to our success—we must strive for excellence in everything we do: in our products, in their safety and value—and in our services, our human relations, our competitiveness, and our profitability.
>
> Employee involvement is our way of life—we are a team. We must treat each other with trust and respect.
>
> Dealers and suppliers are our partners—the company must maintain mutually beneficial relationships with dealers, suppliers, and our other business associates.
>
> Integrity is never compromised—the conduct of our company worldwide must be pursued in a manner that is socially responsible and commands respect for its integrity and for its positive contributions to society. Our doors are open to men and women alike without discrimination and without regard to ethnic origin or personal beliefs.

In addition to their equivalent of mission and operating philosophy statements, most excellent companies have what they specifically refer to as a vision statement. This describes the state of the company in five or ten years. The purpose of this picture is to provide direction for their strategies.

As an example consider Aisin Seiki, which is a member of the Toyota group of companies and winner of the Deming Prize in 1972, the Japanese Quality Prize in 1977 and 1990 (eligible to Deming Award winners five years later), and the Total Productive Maintenance Award in 1982. Aisin Seiki's visions for its past 25 years of TQ have been as follows:

Year	**Vision**
1975	Establishment of quality assurance and improvement of a mass product in structure
1980	Shift from a quantity orientation to a quality orientation/customer focus

1985	Move toward a firm corporate structure
1990	Become a global corporation with connections throughout the world

Mission, operating philosophy, and vision are related in the following way.

Mission (explains the scope of the business and why the business exists)
- ↳ Operating philosophy; also called credo (explains how the values, beliefs, guiding principles, and mission will be followed)
  - ↳ Vision of the business (provides strategic direction in five to ten years)
    - ↳ Strategy (explains how the vision will be attained)
      - ↳ Long-range plans (three to five years)
        - ↳ Annual plan (execute the strategy)
          - ↳ Financial plan (budget)

A draft of the mission and vision statement should be shared with the next lower organizational level after persons at that level have had an educational experience equivalent to top management's. Reactions to this draft should be solicited and considered. The draft must be cascaded in this way to each organizational level. When there is a critical mass of commitment to the draft, it can be made official.

The primary purpose of the vision statement is to provide the basis for evaluating strategies, plans, decisions, and behaviors. The vital question to ask is "Is it consistent with our vision?" The process to create a vision is tremendously educational. The process to develop consensus among a critical mass of leadership will build commitment to TQ.

The next step is to develop a change strategy to attain the vision and an action plan to execute the strategy. The strategy essentially deals with how quickly and in what way the company wants to introduce TQ into the organization. Many companies want to begin by giving the functional areas some exposure to the quality improvement process so they can get their feet wet. Consequently, they initiate pilot projects in each of their major functional areas. In other companies, the internal or external factors might dictate that a company attain world-class competency in several years or face extinction. As a result, these companies might decide to win the Malcolm Baldrige National Quality Award in four years.

Several Japanese companies have used their attainment of the Deming Prize to create a tremendous sense of urgency for their implementation process. Mazda, Kansai Electric, and Yokogowa Hewlett-Packard (YHP) each won the Deming Prize approximately four years after they decided to implement TQ. YHP went from having the highest defect rate and lowest profits of any Hewlett-Packard business unit to having the lowest defect rate and highest profits in those four years.

The action plans specify who is going to do what by a specified date. They provide enough detail to ensure adequate project management. Action plans address the following areas.

1. Improvement projects. Ideally, pilot projects should have a fairly high probability of succeeding within three to five months. They should be done in areas where management is enthusiastic. Having a pilot in the engineering department to apply the new engineering methods is highly recommended because of the enormous leverage to improve the business. Most U.S. companies start in manufacturing. Although TQ must be implemented everywhere, two-thirds of the overall opportunity is in engineering.
2. Changing the infrastructure, which requires the following elements.
   a. An organization to ensure that TQ implementation efforts don't get pushed aside by day-to-day rigors. Most companies call this a quality steering committee or council. This group, which is usually comprised of the top manager and his or her staff,

facilitates, coordinates, and celebrates the implementation process. There also may be a full-time TQ director who is a member of this council who fills the lead facilitation role. Some companies choose not to form a steering committee in order to emphasize that the line organization must lead TQ implementation and to avoid the tendency for top management to delegate this effort and to separate quality management from business management.

b. An ongoing education and training team to develop an integrated architecture for TQ-related educational and job-specific training.
c. A communication team to design a communication process to promote and keep all constituencies of the businesses informed about the TQ implementation process.
d. A performance-measurement team to design a process to ensure that performance measurements are consistent with TQ principles.
e. A rewards/recognition/celebration team to ensure consistency in TQ principles.
f. An assessment team to design a process to assess the TQ implementation efforts relative to the plan. This assessment should be done yearly and should be used to develop the company's annual strategic plan. The assessment process must be led by the CEO and involve management. Including external resources in this process can provide objectivity. Many companies use the Malcolm Baldrige National Quality Award criteria to provide the assessment standard for what is world-class.

Variations of the General Implementation Process

Variation #1. Initiate some pilot improvement projects after management has had only initial exposure to the principles and improvement processes and tools (that is, only about 24 hours of education). Pilot projects can then be executed in parallel with the rest of management's education efforts in preparation for the mission/vision/planning session. Executing pilot projects this early in the implementation process has the following advantages.

1. It helps increase understanding and thereby facilitates the planning session.
2. It can demonstrate benefits early on, which furthers the commitment to do more.
3. It can generate cost savings that can be reinvested in further implementation efforts. In other words, benefits can to some degree fund the implementation process.

The big pitfall in pilot activities is a tendency to make the scope too big and to set expectations too high. This causes frustration and gets the process off to a bad start, which can be hard to overcome in highly skeptical organizations.

Variation #2. Initiate the process with an assessment of the company relative to a standard for a world-class quality process such as the Malcolm Baldrige National Quality Award criteria. The assessment can be made in collaboration with a third party to ensure objectivity. This approach can really get the attention of some entrenched managers who feel that the company's quality and management process are already at or near a world-class level.

Variation #3. Initiate the process with any or all of the following three activities, if they have not been done recently.

1. A study to estimate the cost of quality
2. An assessment of external customers' needs and of their perceptions of the company and its competitors to meet those needs
3. An assessment of internal customer needs

Surveys of employee attitudes and their readiness to change are important elements of an assessment of internal customer needs.

All of these initiatives can help demonstrate that there is an opportunity for improvement. This will justify the investment of time and energy in implementing TQ.

Variation #4. Initiate the process by ensuring that the existing best practices are standardized throughout the organization. Many companies have as many ways to perform a given process as there are individuals involved. Therefore, very significant benefits can be gained by agreeing on the best method and by ensuring that all persons use the same method. Another advantage of starting this way is that it provides a foundation for replicating subsequent process improvements throughout the organization. Although widespread standardization is highly beneficial, it requires a high degree of leadership commitment that might not exist in the initial stage of TQ implementation. Unfortunately, standardization seems to have a bad connotation with many U.S. companies. A large number of organizations feel standardization is mundane and only want to innovate. Tragically, gains from innovation can be quickly lost without a process to hold the gains.

An excellent way to begin standardization in a manufacturing company is to implement what the Japanese call the "five S's", which are:

1. *Seiri*—organization; removing all materials, tooling, gauges, etc., from the work area that are unnecessary.
2. *Seiton*—neatness; having a place for everything and everything in its place.
3. *Seiso*—cleaning; ensuring that everything is clean so that it is ready for use. Cleaning is viewed as a form of inspection.
4. *Seiketsu*—standardization; having everyone use the current best practice.

5. *Shitsuke*—discipline; everyone has the capability (through training) and the will to do what needs to be done.

Some companies have a sixth "S", for safety, to ensure that the five S's are accomplished in a way that ensure a safe environment. Integrating safety is a powerful way to start in the factory because it is something around which everyone in the company can align.

In addition to standardization, the quality and productivity gains from implementing the five S's alone are usually considerable.

Phase 2. Companywide Introduction

In Phase 2 the CEO announces to everyone in the company management's intention to implement TQ, why it's being done, elements of the implementation plan, and the goals (for example, to achieve world-class capability by a given year).

There should be a one- to two-hour educational overview for all employees that introduces the principles and explains the general approach to implementation, including what the pilot projects will be and the issues they will address.

This phase also includes the following activities.

1. Development of a cadre of internal resources for the change process such as trainers and facilitators. The primary purpose of facilitators is to help managers lead in the new way by giving them feedback. Furthermore, facilitators ensure that the quality improvement process is followed and used to address the teams' objective. If the leader guides in the right way, facilitators are not needed. Over the long haul, facilitators work themselves out of a job, but become extremely valuable to the corporation as a result of their experience.

2. Execution of the pilot projects.
3. Establishment of the change infrastructure teams, which will work in parallel with the pilot improvement projects.
4. Initiation of an ongoing, external and internal customer needs assessment processes.
5. Initiation of a process to ensure that success is replicated throughout the company. As the pilot teams begin to realize successes, the steering committee must initiate this process.

All of these efforts are under the care and tutelage of the steering committee, which will hold periodic reviews of progress. A key success factor is that the leadership role models demonstrate the desired leadership behavior and use the quality improvement process in their daily work as well as in structural quality improvement activities. Therefore, it is critical that structured management quality activities have a facilitator to provide feedback to management.

Phase 3. Implementation of a Proactive, Prevention-Based Approach on Critical Business Systems

Phase 3 entails the creation of process improvement teams for critical business systems and applying the quality improvement process. Critical business systems typically include

- External and internal needs assessment and measurement
- Product/service and process development
- Translating customer needs into appropriate quality characteristics and process control plans
- Billing
- Education
- Employee selection
- Recognition and rewards

- Competitive information
- Strategic planning
- Communication
- Sales marketing
- Performance measurement/rewards/promotion
- Career planning and execution
- New employee orientation

The work of the process improvement teams will include benchmarking the company's process against the world's best processes to find characteristics that can make the company's process even better than the world's best. In this phase the improvement team will have redesigned and implemented at least one iteration of a prevention-based approach and will have replicated this redesign throughout the firm. By the end of Phase 3, improvement efforts will be well integrated and, to a large degree, efforts in the company will be focused on the customer.

Phase 4. Institutionalized Continuous Process Improvement on All Major Business Systems

In Phase 4 the company will have implemented for all critical business systems a process to continually improve the proactive, prevention-based approaches applied during Phase 3. There will be demonstrated evidence that these prevention-based business processes will have been refined at least once or twice. That is, the PDCA wheel will have been turned at least once or twice on all critical business processes.

Almost all persons will be involved in ongoing education and process improvement efforts. On the average, education and process improvement activities will account for approximately 10 percent of budgeted or planned head count.

Breakthrough improvement objectives will be deployed throughout the organization after sufficient analysis, input, and commitment by those persons who must achieve the objectives. There will be an ongoing review process to ensure that improvement initiatives are integrated and not out-prioritized by the day-to-day business activities.

Key suppliers will be committed to, and will be implementing, a TQ process. They will be involved intimately in product and/or service design efforts. When processes are improved, the new process standard is replicated throughout the entire organization.

Phase 5. Threshold to World-Class Results

In Phase 5 the company will be a market leader in the products and/or services that it provides. Critical business processes will be at or near a world-class level as determined by an ongoing competitive benchmarking process.

Business systems in all major areas and most support areas will have shown sustained improvement for at least three years. There will be clear evidence that the improved results were due to quality initiatives. In essence, the vision created for the business is now the mind-set of all employees.

Figure 2.1 shows a comparison of some traditional and world-class benchmarks that are applicable to most businesses. Table 2.1 summarizes the five phases of implementation. The horizontal arrows represent the major components of the change infrastructure, which must be established during Phase 1 and continued throughout all subsequent phases.

Critical Success Factors

In our work with many companies in a variety of industries, we have observed the following critical success factors and pitfalls.

1. *Humility*. Without humility, there will be little real learning and change. Without it, listening to and

	Traditional	World-Class
Rejects, errors as percentage of opportunities for error	1–2%	<0.00034%
Customer promises kept	70–85%	>99.9+%
Telephone rings	4–8	≤2
Price of nonconformance as percentage of sales	20–50%	3–5%
Persons contributing ideas	5–10%	95–100%
Average ideas generated per person per year	1/2–1	30–100
Number of ideas implemented	15–25%	85–95%
Time budgeted for education/training and process improvement	0–1%	10%
Absenteeism	3–7%	1–2%
Annual employee turnover	5–40%	<2%

Figure 2.1: Critical differences between traditional and world-class TQ companies in key benchmark areas.

empathizing with external and internal customers will be greatly impaired. According to Yoshinori Iizuka, a JUSE counselor, QC begins with confession of the way things really are and of what problems really exist.. Confession requires humility. The favorite saying of Ray Kroc, the founder of McDonald's, is especially appropriate: "When you're green you grow. When you're ripe you rot."

2. *Commitment to continuous learning for all employees, especially the leadership*. Improved products and services

PHASE 1	PHASE 2
Leadership education, involvement, and planning	Companywide introduction
■ Understand and personally apply quality concepts and improvement methodology ■ Be personally involved in competitively benchmarking a critical business process ■ Create a consensus vision of the future state (that is, values, beliefs, principle of how the firm will operate) ■ Develop a change strategy to achieve the vision ■ Develop a quality plan to execute the strategy. The plan includes the following change infrastructural elements: ■■ Organization ■■ Education ■■ External and internal customer needs assessment ■■ Communication ■■ Performance measurement ■■ Rewards/recognition/celebration	■ CEO announces to the firm the operatin[g] committee's intentions; why do it, elements of the plan, implementation goals (for example, attain a world-class capability by 12/96) ■ Establish change infrastructure ■ Provide an education overview for all fir[m] members ■ Execute pilot projects ■ Develop internal resources (trainers and facilitators) for the change process ■ Initiate external and internal customer needs assessment and measurement process ■ Begin to replicate successful results throughout the firm; standardize the best processes

Table 2.1. The five phases of total quality management implementation.

PHASE 3	PHASE 4	PHASE 5
Implementation of a prevention-based approach on business processes	Culture of continuous process improvement	World-class results
■ Benchmark versus world's best processes ■ Redesign and implement at least one iteration of a prevention-based approach ■ Deploy throughout the firm ■ All improvement efforts/changes are integrated	■ A process to continually improve/refine critical business is in place ■ Demonstrated evidence of refined business processes (one or two iterations of improvement) ■ All persons involved at least 10% of the time in education and process improvement ■ Policy deployment throughout all organizational levels ■ Process improvements replicated throughout the organization	■ World-class performance verified through the competitive benchmarking process ■ Sustained improvement for at least three years ■ Evidence that improved results were due to quality improvement initiatives ■ Vision of the future state is the mind-set ■ Develop more aggressive targets for the future

Internal change resources (facilitators and trainers)

Ongoing and continuously improving education and training process

Ongoing and continuously improving customer needs assessment/measurement process

Ongoing and continuously improving communication process

Ongoing and continuously improving performance measurements

Ongoing and continuously improving reward systems

follow from improved business processes, which in turn follow from the improved capability of people. Improving people is synonymous with learning. Kaoru Ishikawa, recognized as one of the great fathers of the TQ movement in Japan, said that total quality starts and ends with education. One of the best ways to learn a subject is to have to teach it. Therefore, having each management level train those who report to it is a powerful technique to ensure management education.

3. *Intense sense of purpose/mission beyond making profits.* Implementing TQ to a world-class degree requires a huge commitment from everyone in the entire organization, from the top floor to the shop floor. The degree of commitment required will come only if people believe that they are contributing to making the world a better place. The entire TQ effort must tap into this basic human need.
4. *Role modeling and impassioned active involvement by the leadership.* People take their cue from what leaders do, not by what they say. Most top managers greatly underestimate the degree to which they set the tone. Top management must
   - Personally introduce TQ, not just approve its introduction
   - Initiate and be involved in planning for TQ implementation and not appoint someone else to do it
   - Be personally involved in process improvement activities
   - Use the quality improvement process in their daily work
   - Be personally involved in evaluating the implementation process, not just its results
5. *Structured review process integrated with the current business review, with quality always being first on the agenda*
6. *Reward systems that are consistent with TQ principles*
7. *Willingness to deal with recalcitrant managers.* There is a

variation in just about everything in life, including the reaction to good ideas. We have observed that the reaction to TQ by the management groups usually follows the distribution shown.

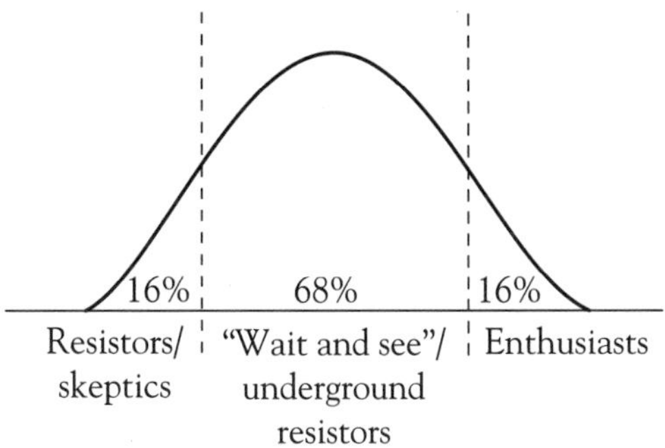

Approximately 15 percent of management will typically resist TQ at the start. Managers must be expected to apply the quality improvement process to some degree. But what is the appropriate level of expectation? How much time should they be given to get involved with the process? Should the lack of attainment of a numerical improvement goal be the trigger for taking action to replace them?

We believe that, initially, it is fair to expect improvement but not full attainment of specific quantitative improvement goals. The key trigger should be whether or not the manager is using the quality improvement methodology and is making a fair attempt. If not, the manager eventually must be removed. TQ implementation requires a totally committed management. When this must be done, the reason for removal must be made public. When management is open about the reason for the change, then the overall level of trust and commitment to TQ will increase drastically.

Start by reinforcing the effective enthusiasts. Many will get the picture and get on board. Let the skeptics, however, express themselves without fear of reprisal.

Chris Fosse, vice president of quality for Omark Industries (later purchased by Blount—one of the first U.S. companies to implement TQ to a significant degree), offers his insights on this issue: "I think you can make improvement faster, more painlessly by working with the 'enthusiasts' and changing the implementation process drivers rather than sorting out the 'defects'. The defects go away eventually."

8. *Stability of leadership*. The cultural change process required by the implementation of TQ is extremely sensitive to top management's consistent leadership. Robert Galvin of Motorola and Roger Milliken are outstanding examples of how stable leadership fosters a culture of continuous improvement. Several companies have made significant progress only to regress when the top management champion leaves. The clear lesson learned is that the persons who decide who will be top management must themselves become committed to TQ so that they can ensure a succession of TQ champions. Dr. Deming refers to this lesson as "creating a constancy of purpose."

Pitfalls

1. *Insufficient time to work on improvement*. The old adage, "When you're up to your neck in alligators, it's tough to remember that your objective is to drain the swamp!" applies to all businesses. This is precisely the challenge—to simultaneously do the job and improve the way the job is done.

Many managers who are already working 60 hours a week wonder where they are going to find the time to "do" TQ. For a time there is no way around the need to work more. Once managers learn to think statistically, however, they'll save between 25 and 33 percent of the time that they previously spent working, because they will stop treating all variation as if it were due to special causes. In other words, they'll stop overreacting.

Even after managers learn to think statistically, it still will be difficult not to let the day-to-day rigors out-prioritize improvement. The organization will need to learn to discipline itself to make improvement as important as everything else—and to focus improvement efforts on the vital few.

2. *Trying to accomplish too much improvement.* Although related to the first pitfall, this one relates specifically to trying to implement too many, or too complex, improvement projects. Many companies start by trying to solve huge, chronic problems that involve many functional areas. Don't be obsessed by heroic goals—just demonstrate continuous improvement. We suggest that you think big but start small. To the greatest possible degree, limit the scope so that projects can be solved primarily by one functional area. This is not contrary to moving quickly, but it does require intense self-discipline and a commitment to building the process step by step. After the functional areas have some experience with the quality improvement process, projects can be gradually made multifunctional.
3. *Letting newly initiated improvement teams select their own leader.* If the team selects a leader whom management has not already legitimized as a leader, that is, someone who's already a manager or supervisor, then it could be extremely threatening to the legitimized leader.

Although there are exceptions, we suggest, as a general rule, that companies start with the formal organization leader and evolve over time to having a nonmanager as a team leader.

4. *Letting newly initiated improvement teams select the improvement project that they will work on.* We suggest that the projects be something that management wants in addition to what the team wants. Otherwise, management won't likely be involved enough to sufficiently coach and encourage the team.
5. *Employees' fear of losing jobs or of not being able to learn the new methods.* Management must issue and enforce a policy that states that no one will lose their job due to improvements, and that if job eliminations are needed, displaced workers will be retrained for other, comparable jobs. Overcoming fear of not being able to learn requires patience and encouragement by management.
6. *Not putting quality first.* Many companies have invested significant resources and energy to implement TQ, but top management has still allowed the shipment of products that weren't right. In such cases, everyone knows that, when push comes to shove, it is still quantity over quality. If management is serious about implementing TQ, it will never compromise quality.
7. *Lack of faith and persistence.* Implementing TQ requires a cultural change and, as Kaoru Ishikawa stated, it is a thought revolution in management. This kind of change requires a high degree of faith and persistence. TQ implementation requires a long-term perspective. Although several Japanese companies made the transformation in about four years, comparably sized American Baldrige Award winners typically have taken about ten years. The intense North American focus on short-term financial returns is probably the single biggest deterrent to long-term TQ progress.

Conclusion

Although all companies that successfully make the transition from traditional to world-class will go through the five basic phases, it is important to remember that there is no one specific approach that is better than the rest. Each company needs to customize its implementation strategy to build upon previous and current change initiatives, degree of TQ understanding and commitment by the leadership, culture, business needs, and leadership style.

Regardless of the approach used, when companies start improvement projects they will need to select where to begin. We strongly encourage that initial efforts include the design area, a point we made in chapter 1. Because much of the leverage for improvement is in engineering, start there as soon as possible. Although all areas of the company need to embrace TQ, if there were only one area in which to start, it is in design engineering. This assertion is probably as valid in most service organizations as it is in manufacturing companies.

Chapters 1 and 2 provided the context for management by policy. Chapters 3 and 4 will describe management by policy in depth. Chapter 5 describes how companies implement a management-by-policy system and will refer to the general discussion of TQ implementation in chapter 2.

3

Elements of Management by Policy

Without vision people are lost.

—Proverbs

Elements of Management by Policy

An old adage says, "You can't tell the players without a program." The same is true when it comes to explaining the direction of an organization. It is difficult to determine the direction unless it is clearly spelled out and made visible to all employees. This is the context in which management by policy is becoming popular in the United States.

Management by policy singles out a few areas, two or three at most (preferably only one at first), that get priority attention for a planned period of time. According to Noriaki Kano, a Deming Award counselor, MBP requires that managers make unhappy decisions; that is, pare down managers' list of initiatives to those significant few that will make a difference and for which there are adequate resources. The organization's efforts and resources are pointed in the direction of these critical areas, and that is where top management's attention is clearly focused. Of course, these are not the only things going on in the organization. Rather, these carefully selected items are pushed to the top of the heap and take on a sense of urgency that comes from concentrated attention by senior management. This June, 1992 Associated Press release reveals one of Nissan's significant few areas of focus.

> NISSAN IS CUTTING DOWN ON
> PARTS TO BOLSTER PROFITS
>
> The Nissan Motor Company of Japan said yesterday that it would save on labor costs by reducing the amount of parts needed in its cars by 30 percent in the next three to five years. Nissan decided on the streamlining in hopes of improving its profitability. The company declined to say how much the plan was expected to save. About 60,000 parts, including nuts and bolts, are now needed to build a vehicle. Nissan said it would design a new model that could easily be produced with fewer parts.

Management by policy (MBP) is a management process to help the company achieve dramatic improvement that supports the corporate vision. The process focuses the resources of the company on a few high-priority issues to achieve breakthrough. *Policy refers to both the objectives and the methods or means to attain the objectives.*

In the context of MBP the word *policy* has a connotation different from what's currently used in most U.S. businesses—even those with mature total quality implementation efforts. For example, one prominent electronics company has what it calls quality policies. One of those policies is for the reliability of every new product model to be at least equal to the reliability of the models they replace and to the models of competitors. Another company has a quality policy that requires new production processes to be turned over to the line manufacturing organization only if they are fully capable (in the statistical sense). Having such quality policies is very appropriate. It is important to distinguish this meaning of policy from that used in MBP.

Historical Perspective

Management by policy was developed from management by objectives (MBO) by total-quality companies. Like many U.S. companies, many Japanese companies implemented MBO in the mid- to late 1960s. As some Japanese companies implemented TQ to an advanced degree, however, they realized that MBO was inconsistent with a number of TQ principles. When these companies exercised the plan-do-check-act cycle on MBO, they helped MBO evolve to MBP.

When the worldwide oil crisis occurred in 1973, the development of MBP received a tremendous boost because it enables a fast, corporatewide response to major, unforeseen world events. Realizing that the frequency of unforeseen world events, such as the energy shortage, is probably going to increase as the world's economy becomes more interrelated, more companies have attempted MBP. But many companies with an otherwise good TQ process still have what amounts to MBO—objectives without the means to accomplish them. The MBP process that we describe is MBP as it has evolved through the application of continuous improvement.

While MBP was originally developed as a defensive capability for dealing with major unforeseen events, it now has evolved into a major offensive weapon. MBP provides the focus, the means, and the driving force for excellent companies that want to dominate worldwide markets.

MBP Versus MBO

Over the years MBP has evolved into something quite different from MBO. Table 3.1 shows some important distinctions.

Management by objectives (MBO)	Management by policy (MBP)
Focus is frequently on the financial objectives of the company only	Focus is on a few major corporate improvements or opportunities
Focus is almost exclusively on company needs	Focus is on customer needs
Focus is on year-end results only	Focus is on processes, means, and results
Basis of individual rewards are given priority	Individual awards are not the driving force
Focus is within each department	Focus is across department lines
Focus is on individual contributions; MBO goes directly from company goals to individual performance objectives	Focus is on strengthening management through the improvement of processes

Table 3.1: Key differences between management by objectives (MBO) and management by policy (MBP).

Essentially, management by policy

- Is obsessed with the customer
- Provides a clear focus on a few major improvements or opportunities
- Provides careful detailed attention to process, means, and results

- Recognizes that most major improvements will require cross-functional cooperation
- Requires a high degree of participation in identifying major improvement objectives or opportunities and the means and resources to achieve them by the people who must achieve the goals

This understanding demands that the senior management team think through the structure of business, identify the drivers, the processes, and the outputs, and—above all—apply logical thinking to the functions for which they are responsible. We would all be very critical if someone were to join a marathon race at the 20-mile marker and then try to take credit for winning. Why should it be any different in business? Why expect that we can manipulate the financials at the end of the race when we have not put in the effort at every step along the way?

Evolution of Management by Policy

When a company attempts to implement management by policy it might go through an evolution rather than a revolution. You can expect to see some of the following transitions, which might be rough and unclear.

First, the idea that there is a serious focus on changing corporate direction and emphasizing dramatic improvements is difficult to make operational.

Second, there is a reluctance to use the Pareto principle. This usually results in an attempt to work on all things that are important, all at the same time. In fact, many managers might fear being perceived as disloyal if they say anything other than "I can do that."

Third, objectives tend to be general and not supported by an analysis of the methods and means of obtaining the targets. Often there is a fear to commit to any kind of quantifiable improvement.

Fourth, the ability to select improvement areas and the improvement targets, based on data, tends to be limited.

Fifth, reviews are rarely seen as opportunities to gain support and garner assistance. Rather they tend to be seen as opportunities to shoot the messenger.

Initially it might be difficult to drive all strategy by an analysis of present and future customer needs. To paraphrase the sentiments of many executives, customer satisfaction focus is okay for the textbooks, but when it comes to the real world of business the primary drivers must be quantity, revenues, and cost.

To make MBP work well, managers must believe that financial performance follows from customer satisfaction, which in turn follows from process improvements. The old belief that the company should be run solely by financial numbers must be disregarded. Until this old belief is replaced by the new one, the transition will be rough.*

The transition from MBO to MBP (see Table 3.2) can be expedited when: (1) the PDCA cycle is applied to the strategic planning and execution process; (2) a serious attempt is made to diagnose the weaknesses in the process from year to year; and (3) the appropriate improvements are made. Ultimately, the process must be driven by analysis that results in the selection of optimum opportunities for dramatic improvement.

Management by Policy and the Big Picture

The first step is to identify and prioritize areas in which dramatic improvement can significantly affect competitiveness. The process should reflect more than the whim of a few executives sitting around a big table expounding on what they feel is important to the future of the company. The process must be guided by a larger dynamic—one that recognizes that effective, expert management requires a powerful and responsive system that not only is structured, disciplined, and focused, but that also is flexible.

*For a superb exposition of the implications of total quality principles in the field of management accounting, see H.T. Johnson, *Relevance Regained*, Free Press, 1992.

MBO stage	Interim stage	Mature MBP stage
Approach is from the company's perspective	Approach is from the company's perspective	Approach is from the customer's perspective
All departments participate without regard to their potential for impact	All departments participate without regard to their potential for impact	Focus on participation; those who can make a major contribution to this improvement effort participate; a prioritized approach for implementation is used
Objectives are general	Objectives are general (indicators and targets might exist but are not required)	Contribution to improvement is based on analysis of methods to obtain objectives; those who can actually impact improvement are brought into alignment
Quarterly status report	Review structures added but are perceived as punitive or an invasion of territory	Review structures are added and are perceived as diagnostic and as an opportunity for support and progress
Focus on quantity and cost	Recognizes customers' needs as important	Emergence of added structure—formalized customer input
Each year is a new beginning and brings a new set of urgent objectives	Problems gleaned from organization (objectives for improvement)	Opportunities for major improvement are determined by analysis of quality systems

Table 3.2: The transition from MBO to mature MBP.

The larger process is generally called a management system. It consists of several processes that are worked on simultaneously by various groups of key people, ranging from the top management team to selected executives to business units and their managers and workers.

There are several criteria for selecting major corporate improvement objectives. The objectives must

- Reflect major opportunity for improvement from the customers' perspective
- Be cross-functional
- Deserve high-level management attention
- Be urgent, such as when a significant threat is encountered.

With the Japanese, the oil shortage in 1973 and extreme currency fluctuations are examples of urgently needed objectives. Both situations provided strong impetus for MBP developmental efforts.

Of course, the ultimate decision is made by senior management. The assumption, however, is that the selections are based on data and that they have been subjected to the kind of analysis that leads to the identification of priority areas (the Pareto process).

Management by Policy—Three Phases

The term *management by policy* is best understood as a label that describes a comprehensive process. It covers the spectrum from identifying the right things to do, all the way to ensuring that those right things are effectively implemented. Management by policy can be summed up as the infrastructure that ensures that the right things are done right, and at the right time.

We will examine the details of the three phases of the MBP process: establish policy, deploy policy, and implement policy. The first phase deals specifically with selecting the right things. It considers the customers' needs, the business environment, the long-term strategy, internal issues, and current performance.

Once the path is selected and the policies established, the deployment phase provides the challenge to ensure that all of the right people are included and that they have a clear picture of what they must do. Those contributors also must have confidence that they are working on the right things at their level. Their targets need to be both challenging and achievable.

The implement phase is possible once the optimum areas for improvement are selected, the appropriate people are on board, the analysis has been done, and the contributions are sufficient to achieve the overall corporate target. Implementation is the only thing that really makes a difference. It requires first-class project management skills as well as effective support through skillful reviews.

Figure 3.1 shows the three phases of management by policy. Each consists of many strands, all of which contribute to an integrated process.

Establish Policy

All the components of the establish-policy phase are in the domain of the senior management team. Many inputs are reviewed to establish policy. Our discussion is not intended to be exhaustive but rather it serves as a starting point to stimulate thinking about an approach that must be customized for each organization.

Assess Customer Needs and Satisfaction Levels

The fundamental premise is that customer satisfaction is the central driving force. Consequently, it is not surprising that the process must start with identifying customer needs and determining customer satisfaction. The response to this might vary from "We already know our customers' needs, so let's stop wasting time" to "Oh no! We have to come up with a million dollars to get the best survey people in the country on board." There is a happy medium. While it is important to ask the customers what they need, it is also

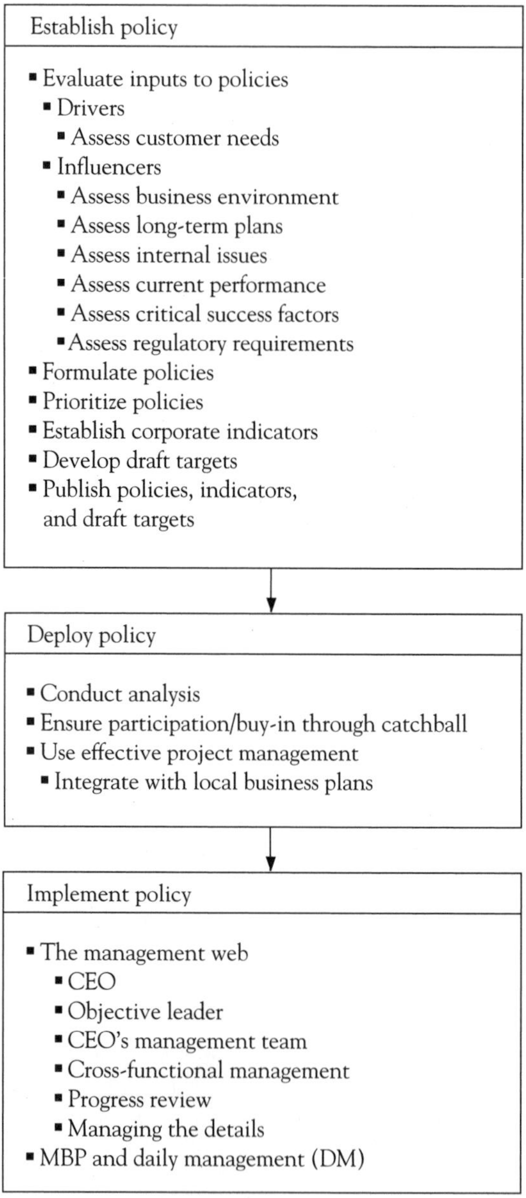

Establish policy

- Evaluate inputs to policies
  - Drivers
    - Assess customer needs
  - Influencers
    - Assess business environment
    - Assess long-term plans
    - Assess internal issues
    - Assess current performance
    - Assess critical success factors
    - Assess regulatory requirements
- Formulate policies
- Prioritize policies
- Establish corporate indicators
- Develop draft targets
- Publish policies, indicators, and draft targets

↓

Deploy policy

- Conduct analysis
- Ensure participation/buy-in through catchball
- Use effective project management
  - Integrate with local business plans

↓

Implement policy

- The management web
  - CEO
  - Objective leader
  - CEO's management team
  - Cross-functional management
  - Progress review
  - Managing the details
- MBP and daily management (DM)

Figure 3.1: The management by policy process.

important to first figure out who the customers are. The complaints records will tell you who the complaining customers are and to some degree probably what their needs are. But don't forget about those who do not make an effort to complain or potential customers who currently buy from a competitor.

Studies show that 95 percent of all dissatisfied customers don't complain. A good way for some companies to start is to interact directly with their significant few customers in a one-on-one setting. Surveys have been useful to many companies. Although a survey is important, it does not have to be perfect on the first try; it can be continuously reviewed and updated as the data base is built over several iterations.

Hearing from the customers is just the beginning. The next step is to take that information and translate it into terminology that is consistent with the jobs that employees actually do.

For example, assume we are in the cookie-making business. When customers tell us that they do not like it when their cookies are crushed when they open the package, we realize that there is no job that is supposed to produce crushed cookies. Rather, there should be processes that produce cookies at a consistency that reduces breakage, that packs them in crush-resistant containers, and that transports them appropriately. Employees will understand these concepts and will be able to figure out what actions must be taken to meet the customers' needs.

The needs of future customers are a different story. The ability to identify these needs requires insights into psychology, sociology, technological developments, and political trends. Reading the future requires more than understanding the past. There is no simple formula that can be plugged in to give a picture of the future. Yet the effort must be made and adjustments must be allowed as old insights are modified and new insights develop.

The customer's voice can be determined through a formal survey, though doing this is usually more difficult than companies initially think. The emphasis is on *formal* because there are certain rules that apply to ensure that the data collected are representative of the customers and are reliable.

Customers' hidden needs are more difficult to get at. They require insight into what excites customers about the product or service that is provided. Focus groups that use open-ended questioning can be one means of getting to those hidden needs. Another method is to have trained observers document customer behaviors.

It is possible to establish a valid perception of real customer needs by blending the process of hearing the customers' voice with that of discovering their hidden needs. Once known, customers' needs are translated into the language of the company and are expressed in terms of major corporate processes, as Figure 3.2a shows. After these corporate processes are determined, it is possible to establish indicators that provide a method of measurement.

Identifying customers and their needs through formal needs assessment processes can take months. Rather than wait for these data, companies can start with customer dissatisfaction data, which are available by aggregating customer complaints.

The major corporate processes can be divided into several categories for ease of management. An example of such a division might be: product/service quality, cost, delivery, safety, and morale/social responsibility (see Figure 3.2b).

Assess the General Business Environment

There are many aspects that need attention in this area. All aspects of the economy must be considered, including the direction of the stock market, interest rates, inflation, and tax laws.

Attention must be paid to market share, changing market conditions, and potential market opportunities. Probably the most critical aspect of the general business situation is the competitive environment. What are the current and anticipated competitive niches? What are the strengths and weaknesses relative to the customers' perceptions of product or service quality and delivery processes?

The political arena also deserves close attention. Consider potential legislative changes at all governmental levels. What is happening in the international arena? What companies factored in

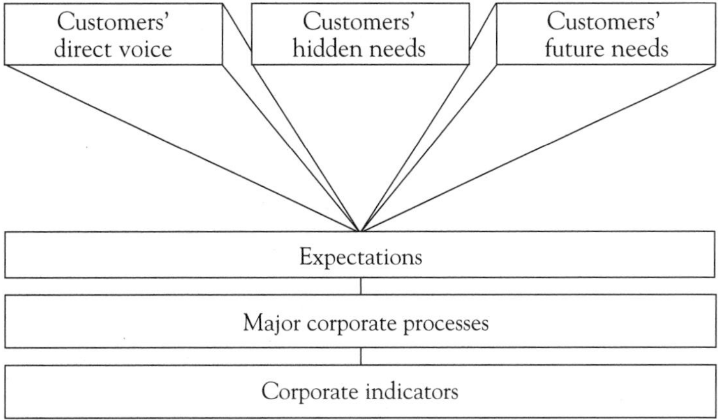

Figure 3.2a: Listening to and deploying customers' needs.

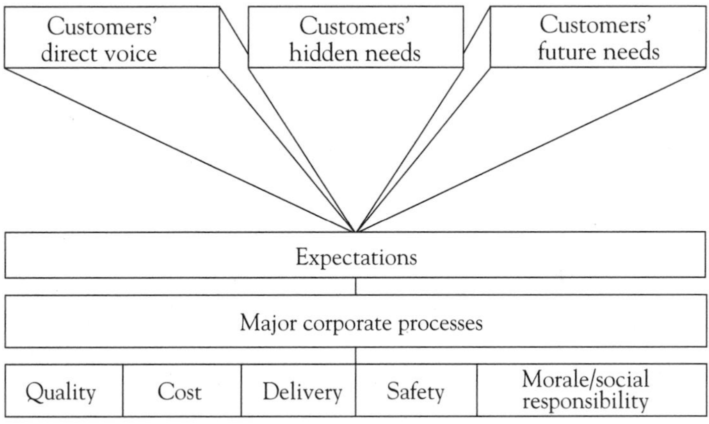

Figure 3.2b: How the various customer voices translate to specific corporate processes.

the changes in Eastern Europe as part of their development of annual policies?

Pending technological changes can also have a great impact on where the company needs to focus its attention. The advent of the microchip opened up a whole new world. What will the next microchip be and how will it influence our business?

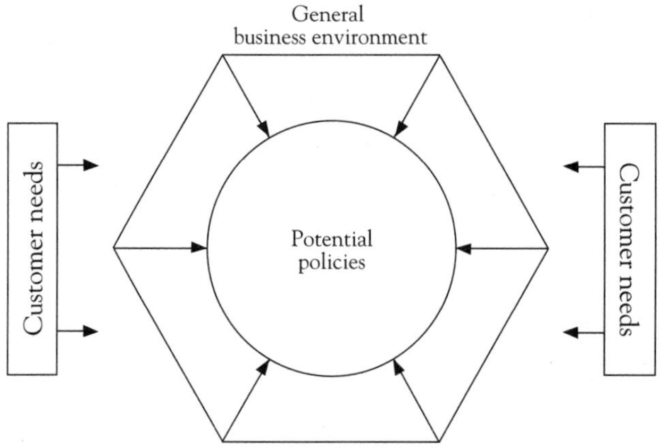

Assess Long-Term Plans

In recent times there has been cynicism about long-term plans. A recent cartoon depicted a short-term plan as something to do before 5:00 P.M. this evening and a long-term plan as a series of short-term plans strung together. Some of this cynicism is justified if long-term plans are viewed as inflexible sets of directions that are protected at the very highest level.

Long-term plans are in the three- to five-year range. They are clearly spelled out, but, contrary to common misconception, they must be flexible, dynamic, and open to quick adaptation to the changing world environment.

Managing long-term plans requires the aggressive attention of the top management team. The input must be based on comprehensive data-driven diagnosis. The reality is that long-term plans might change a little or a lot, frequently or infrequently, depending on what is going on in the world that surrounds them.

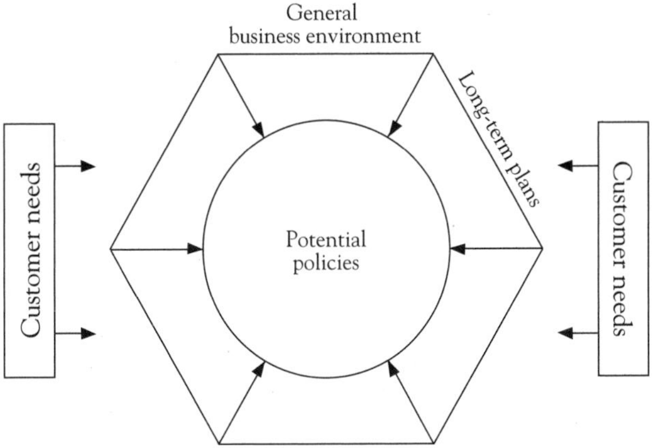

Assess Internal Issues

The aggressive habit of looking around to see what's going on and then translating that into the business plan should not be left strictly to corporate management. It also should be the primary habit of local management thinking. Local issues surface constantly. Frequently these issues can be handled by local management, though to do this they sometimes must be elevated to the local priority list. On occasion, these issues appear to be so daunting as to require corporate focus and attention to ensure successful intervention. Critical processes with chronic problems are examples.

In companies with a mature MBP application, process capability for all critical processes is known and is a vital consideration for establishing policies.

Another important perspective on local issues can be gained from analyzing apparent patterns from diverse locations. This might signal a potentially important trend that is not evident at the corporate level but, when compared with other factors, might indicate a critical emerging issue.

A third aspect related to emerging internal local issues relates to the check-and-balance function. As major corporate processes are improved and deemed capable, it is important to ensure integrated linkages throughout the processes. The bubbling up of local issues might signal failures in processes that were considered capable.

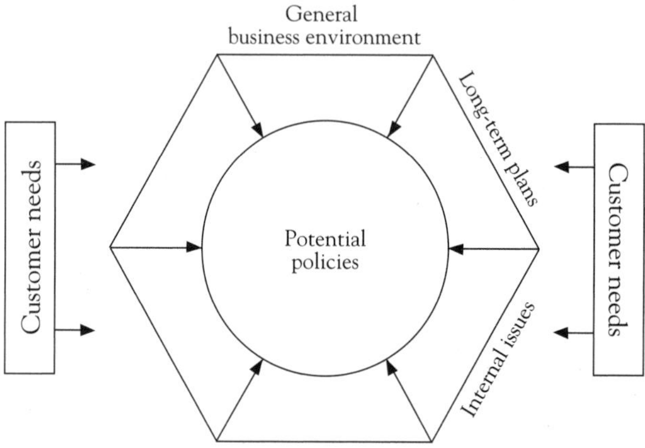

Assess Current Performance

The more sophisticated this planning process becomes, the longer senior management can wait to identify major improvement opportunities for the next year. This in turn allows them to wait until very late in the year to assess current performance. In fact, the later the better, because a more accurate picture of year-end data can be developed.

Sophistication comes in terms of data-driven preparation and analysis taking the place of hunches, opinions, and gut feelings. Good analysis can set up a sequence of opportunities that reflect Pareto consideration and an aggressive pursuit of root causes. In particular, close attention must be paid if the target is not met or exceeded. Either outcome might be a signal for even more aggressive analysis of the gap between desired and actual performance.

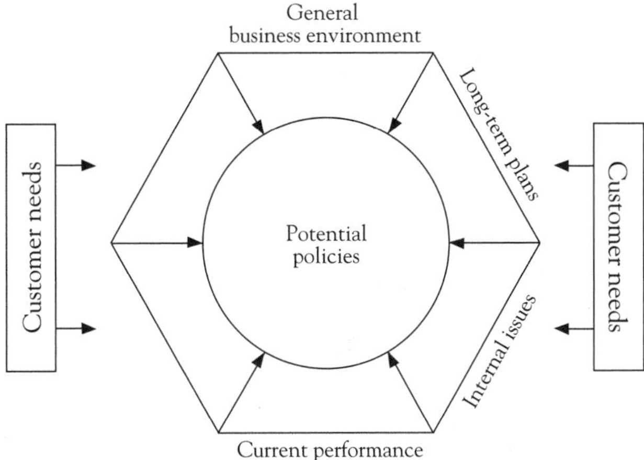

Assess Critical Success Factors

Sensitivity to the aspects of the business that have worked well for others is invaluable. These factors will vary widely from business to business—it is just a matter of doing the homework for any given business.

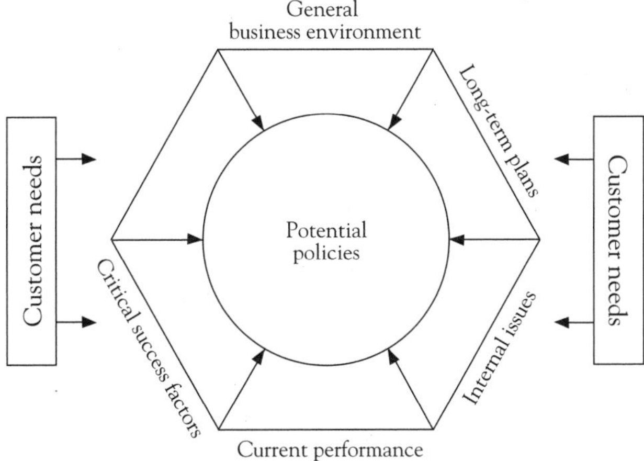

Assess Regulatory Requirements

Every company is regulated in some manner. When regulatory requirements change, timely response is always critical and often expensive. Potential regulation changes must be factored into the development of policy for the coming year.

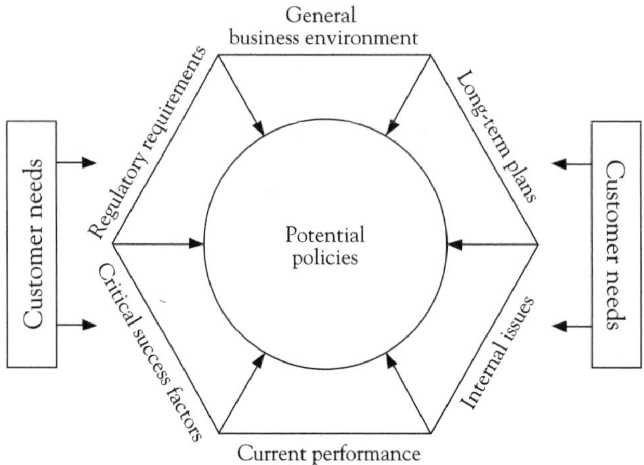

Formulate Policies After Thorough Reflection

Policies are formulated by reflecting upon the inputs and requirements previously discussed. This reflection process varies from company to company. In some cases the senior managers do it as a team, while in others the process starts with the CEO reflecting individually and then sharing ideas with senior managers. At the Japanese company Komatsu, the president takes all of the input with him to a mountain retreat for several weeks of reflection each year. In all companies that are doing MBP well, senior executives are actively involved in this reflection process. Formulating the initial draft of policy is not delegated to a staff planning group.

To facilitate the reflection process, ask the following questions. Having well-thought-out answers will help ensure the quality of the strategic analysis.

1. How will you measure superior value in the future?
2. How do you know what it takes to win?

3. What are the sources of competitive advantage? Of presence? Of market access? Of core competencies? Of work processes? Of organizational structures?
4. What gaps must be bridged? What do you need to be able to do that you're not now doing? What can you stop doing? What processes must be improved?
5. What is the motivating and aligning goal of the organization?

Prioritize Policies

A major challenge facing the senior executive team is to pick the critical few from among the many opportunities that could be pursued. It is easy to say yes to everything that people want to do. The tendency is to want to do everything now rather than accept the discipline of starting with the most critical and then working down the list. As Dr. Kano states, "management's job is to make those unhappy decisions." The Pareto principle is more important for senior executives than it is for a quality circle, since the magnitude of the impact is greater at the corporate level.

The three critical drivers for selecting the few priority areas for dramatic improvement are

1. Importance to the customer
2. Opportunity for competitive advantage
3. Areas that have the greatest need for improvement

Ultimately, the goal is to have the few most critical things clearly identified. There should not be more than two or three priorities. Ideally, companies will start with only one.

After their TQ implementation process is well enough along, some companies select safety, reduction of the cost of quality, and product service improvement as their three overarching objectives. Product improvement typically relates to reducing the concept-to-market cycle. Advanced practitioners of MBP frequently have a major overarching objective for each of the five major categories of customer satisfaction (quality, cost, delivery, safety, and morale/social responsibility).

The following are examples of breakthrough policies for each function of customer satisfaction.

- Quality: Improve product reliability to be the best in the industry through a more integrated design process.
- Cost: Reduce product costs by 30 percent through improved understanding of the voice of the customer, reduced quality costs, and parts reduction.
- Delivery: Increase flexibility to schedule changes through a 20 percent reduction in lead time.
- Safety: Attain a world-class level of safety for all company employees by involving all employees in workplace design.
- Morale: Enhance employee security through improved compensation, training, and business strategy.

Establish Corporate Indicators

Once the critical area for improvement has been selected, it is important to determine how progress will be measured. The method of measurement is called an *indicator*. An indicator or measurement of an important output of a process is sometimes called a *control point*.

For example, an important output of a biochemical process is yield percentage. A measurement of an important process parameter (one that affects the output) is sometimes called a *checkpoint*. In the biochemical process shown in Figure 3.3, time, temperature, pressure, acidity, quantity, and quality of ingredients are important process parameters.

Develop Draft Targets

The improvement target communicates the degree of change required. Developing targets frequently causes discomfort for several reasons. There can be a reluctance on the part of those who work in

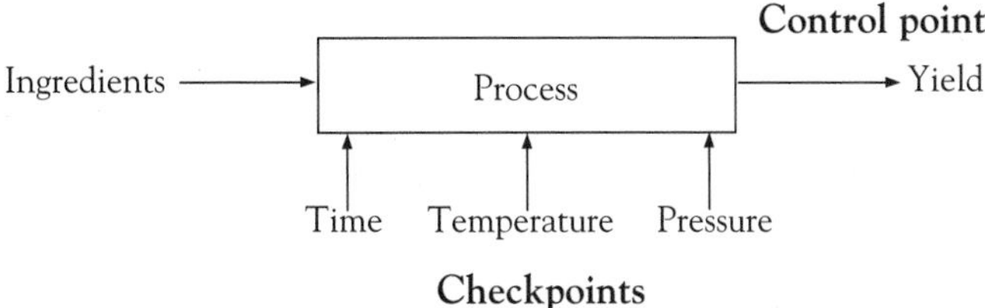

Figure 3.3: Key parameters of a biochemical manufacturing process.

the process to be pinned down to a concrete number, a level of improvement that must be pursued. The reluctance might be the outcome of not wanting to be held accountable, or it might be the result of not having conducted an analysis that is thorough enough to substantiate the desired goal.

Why select a draft target? It is the result of the best analysis available from the corporate perspective. It may not have the benefit of local analysis or the identification of capability of local processes. Furthermore, acceptance of the target must be bolstered by the buy-in—both up and down the organizational ladder—of those who will be expected to bring about the necessary changes.

The traditional approach has been described as deployment of targets. In companies with the best MBP processes, all management levels consider customer requirements and the company's situation compared to competitors. The CEO starts the next step with a draft of policies (targets and means). Each management level takes the input from the level above and responds in an iterative process, which is very much both top-down and bottom-up. This aspect of MBP probably best distinguishes it from what has been done in the past. In the traditional approach a target is arbitrarily selected at the executive level, and a directive is then given to the lower levels as to what their contribution will be. This approach fails to consider the analysis required to determine the capability of the processes. It also ignores the importance of ownership by those who will actually do the work.

There are other considerations in establishing draft targets. An analysis of direct competitors provides a good sense of how the company stands compared to others. Competitive benchmarking—comparisons of results and methods with the best in the world, whether or not they are direct competitors—gives even greater insight. Competitive benchmarking explains many of the whys as well as the differences themselves. Other issues such as the influence of new technology, possible changes in regulatory requirements, and changing customer expectations must also be considered.

Targets must not be picked arbitrarily. They must be based on valid, data-driven insights that will ensure improvements that will make a difference in the eyes of the customers.

Finally, as targets are selected, it is important that the sense of urgency for this particular improvement does not get in the way of other equally important improvements. Creating a sense of balance between the several very important areas of focus is essential to the ultimate success of a company.

Publish Policies, Indicators, and Draft Targets

The policies, indicators, and draft targets should be published companywide well in advance of the budgeting process. This should be done so that the areas singled out for dramatic improvement are highly visible to everyone. It also will allow those who will be most affected to complete the analysis and identify the improvement actions that must be implemented to achieve the corporate target.

Analysis includes resource requirements. Implementation of the improvement actions must be moved to the top of the list in the business plan, which means that the resources to ensure implementation are also given top priority. The following schematic reflects the appropriate sequence of various activities.

Mission—why the business exists—scope of business
- Operating philosophy or credo—explains values, beliefs, and guiding principles
  - Vision—provides strategic direction to attain the mission; five to ten years in the future
    - Strategy—to attain the vision
      - Long-range plan—to execute strategy; five to ten years
        - Medium-range plan—two to five years
          - Annual plan/policies—includes improvement and maintenance actions
            - Financial plan/budget

Deploy Policy

There is often confusion about how management by policy differs from other management practices. The differences are subtle but substantial. In the past, many companies invested a lot of energy identifying annual objectives. You might remember that those objectives often reflected desired earnings, proposed staff reductions, and conformance to budget. These are not the kind of objectives you find when the management by policy process is used.

Management by policy focuses on dramatic improvements or opportunities in the quality of products and services, in cost, in delivery, in safety, and in morale/social responsibility. This focus comes from paying attention to expressed customer needs and from knowing how the company's performance affects what is important to the customer. There is an assumption that budgets are properly constructed and that they will be met. Furthermore, there is an assumption that earnings are the result of doing the right things right—and that all of the exhortation and wishing in the world is not enough if the right things are not done right.

But perhaps the area of greatest contrast is in the deployment of policy. This is a highly disciplined process that is built around several key concepts.

Analysis

The scientific method is the approach used. Consistency of direction is ensured through analysis, and clear linkage from top to bottom is established. The top-level objective merely points toward an opportunity. To get to the next level, the question "Why is this a problem or opportunity?" must be answered. This process of questioning is followed down through the organization to the furthest point possible. Analysis is finding the answer to the question "Why?" This analysis becomes the thread that connects the strands of deployment into a single, tightly woven fabric. Good analysis requires that answers be supported by facts and data.

It is not by accident that when first-level supervisors in a mature MBP system are asked to identify what corporate priority they support and what contributions they make to the total improvement, they can easily articulate their efforts. They have been involved in the iterative communication process called *catchball* and their contribution was identified through analysis rather than through guesswork.

Appropriate target setting is another key component of analysis. The teachings of Dr. Deming are beginning to have some impact on management thinking in the United States. Dr. Deming deals very effectively with the use of arbitrary measures. He points out how dangerous this approach can be, particularly since it can have an adverse effect on those who are attempting to respond to the measures, but who do not realize that the processes are not capable of ever accommodating this level of achievement.

Unfortunately, Deming's message has been interpreted by some to mean that objectives and targets are contrary to good quality improvement thinking. Targets are essential to quality improvement, but must be the product of extensive analysis that considers the urgency of the improvement from the customer's point of view, process capability, the resources available to support the effort, and the priority of the effort compared to other competing priorities. This is quite different from arbitrary imposition of a required contribution based on the whim of someone who has not used catchball and has not participated in answering the question "Why?" at every level.

The analysis component of management by policy is at the core of all that is different in this process. This is the step that ensures that the real barriers or opportunities are identified. It represents the step beyond wishing for answers, guessing at causes, and speculating about what might be. It withstands the rigors of cause-and-effect analysis, moving beyond symptoms to identifiable sustained causes. Analysis is, in effect, the plan step in the PDCA cycle. Only after analysis are solutions considered. Any proposed fixes will be tested to ensure that they are the right choices.

Ultimately when actions are selected they can be implemented with confidence. The means for bridging the gap between existing and desired performance have been effectively identified. There is a high level of confidence that the expected results can be achieved. We suggest the following guideline: there must be consensus that there is a high probability that the means will accomplish the objective.

Catchball

Catchball is an iterative process of developing objectives and plans to obtain the objectives, sharing them with persons who must execute the plans, requesting and considering their input, and finalizing the objectives and plans after sufficient involvement and commitment by all affected parties. Catchball is effective two-way communication that results in joint commitment and joint ownership.

The process of catchball is probably best understood by actually trying it out. When you toss a ball to someone, taking care to ensure that the ball can be caught, there is a good chance that it will be caught. The receiver knows that the ball is coming, that the throw is accurate and careful, and that there will be no surprises. This strengthens the confidence of the receiver and greatly increases the chance of a reception.

The same care and attention must be paid to an objective for improvement when it is deployed down through an organization. The attention and care required to ensure that it is caught at the next level is more than issuing a memo or saying "I announced it at my staff meeting."

There is a saying, "What I thought I said is not what they thought they heard." This sums up the difficult task of passing on the desired direction from one level to another. We all know how difficult it is to maintain a consistent message down through each layer of the organization. Effective project management is the next step on the road to management by policy.

Effective Project Management

By the time we reach this stage, the areas selected for deployment are not just best guesses; they are the product of clear problem or opportunity identification. They are the result of stringent analysis of data leading to precise problem definition at the macro level. Furthermore, stratification has been conducted to identify the areas that have the greatest impact on this corporate problem or opportunity. The owners of those areas of impact will have followed a similar process at their level leading to local problem statements, objectives for improvement, analysis, and appropriate improvement actions.

The deployment phase of MBP starts with the establishment of control points for an overarching objective and then cascading these objectives and means into a series of interrelated control points and checkpoints throughout the organization. Good objectives, regardless of their level, will include targets. The means at one level become the objectives at the next lower management level as shown in Figure 3.4.

The abbreviated example of a manufacturing company in Figure 3.5 shows how objectives and means are cascaded throughout the organization.

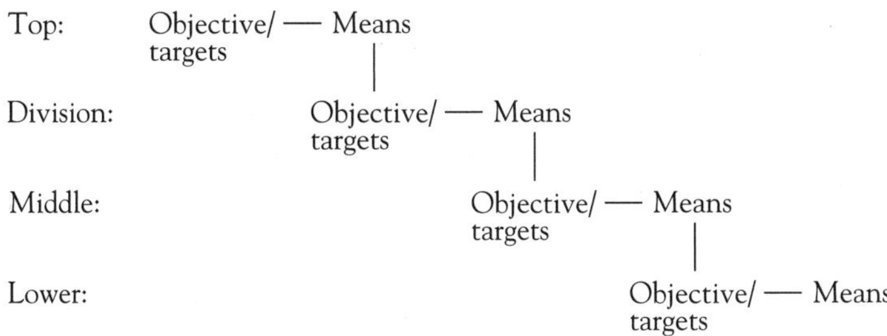

Adapted from Masaaki Imai, Kaizen, *1986.*

Figure 3.4: The interrelationship of objectives/targets and means.

Figure 3.6 shows how the sequence of events unfolds in an example of a utility company. You can see from these examples that each level within the organization must play an active role leading to the identification of specific projects that are selected for quantifiable contributions. The discipline of project management ensures that each detail gets appropriate attention. One method of keeping tabs is in the reporting format shown in Figure 3.7.

The attention to detail is a common thread found in every aspect of management by policy. This is a far cry from scrambling, blaming, and looking for scapegoats. Attending to details is the true test of a leadership that is serious about results. It brings focus and alignment, which lead to lasting improvement. Think for a moment of a large rock. The mission is to move that rock quickly, but, because of unclear directions, each individual is pushing as hard as possible without knowing what the others are doing.

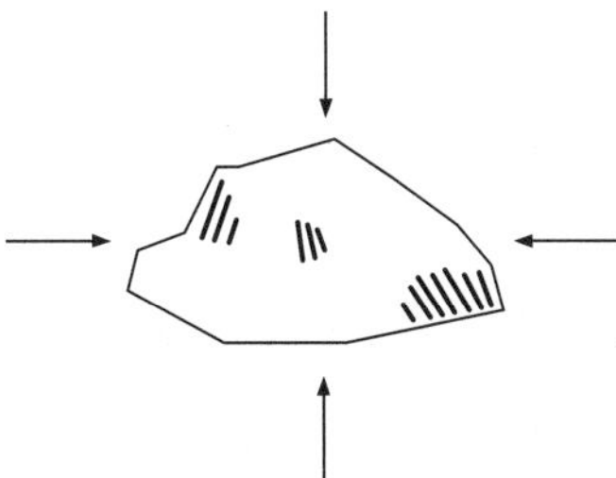

	Objective/target →	Means
Top management	Reduce customer order lead time by 50%	• Production control by 50% • Sales by 40% • Manufacturing by 20%

Department	Objective/target →	Means
• Production control	Reduce by 50%	Implement an on-line order acceptence and control system
• Sales	Reduce by 40%	1. Improve the order form 2. Provide additional training
• Manufacturing	Reduce by 20%	1. Implement a product-focused cell for product ABC 2. Reduce set-up times to 10 minutes or less 3. Increase machine availability to 95% by having operators perform routine maintenance
• Engineering		Redesign product ABC to be modular so that customer orders can be built to order in final assembly
• Human resources		Finalize new work rules with the union to allow operators to perform routine maintenance

Figure 3.5: A manufacturing company example of how the means to achieve a specific objective (reduce customer order time by 50 percent) are cascaded throughout the organization.

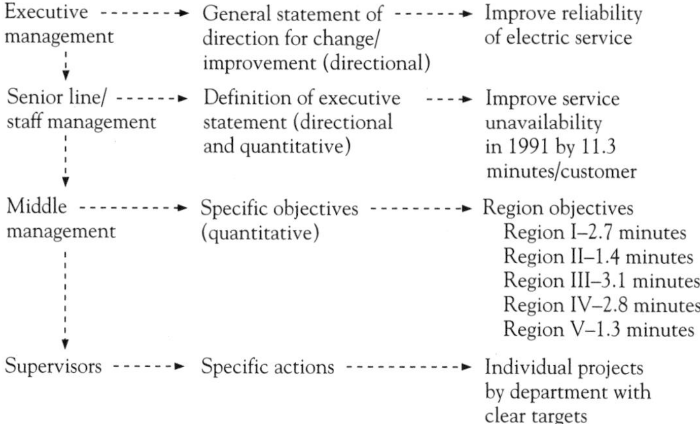

Figure 3.6: Deployment of policy in a utility company.

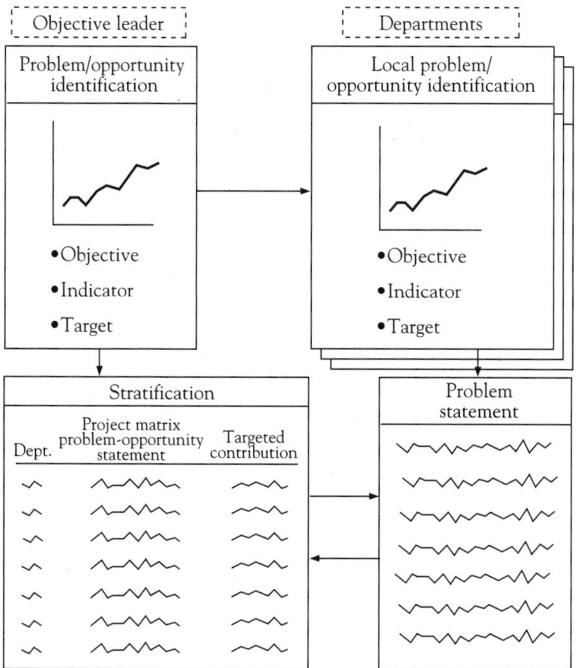

Figure 3.7: Reporting format for ensuring that each element of policy deployment gets appropriate attention.

Now consider what happens when directions are clear; alignment and cooperation take the place of individual interest and all push in the same direction.

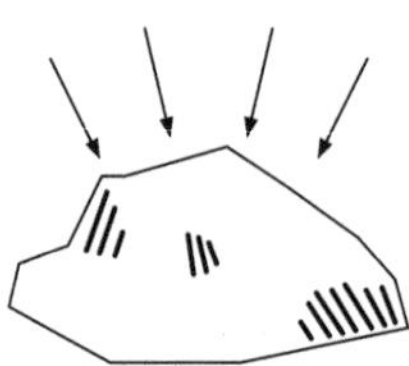

The results are dramatic and ultimately the effort is much less strenuous over the long haul.

Implement Policy

It might seem that a lot of effort has been expended getting to implementation, but much effort is required to develop and deploy policies that will ensure that the right things are implemented. Only if Phases 1 and 2 are done correctly will there be opportunity for success. Implementation won't overcome planning errors. Even with significant prior effort, implementation is not automatic. It requires ongoing management of each improvement and opportunity action as well as the implementation of all of the pieces. Chapter 4 will provide a detailed discussion of the various components that ensure effective implementation.

4

Implementing Policy

Separate the vital few from the trivial many.

—J. M. Juran

For policy to be implemented effectively, several pillars must be firmly in place. These pillars are linked by a framework that we will call the *management web*.

The Management Web

To facilitate the discussion of the implement policy step, visualize the management-by-policy system as the spinning of a web. Its structure is intricate and delicate. It can be easily broken, and without close care and attention it can become an entangled mess. It does not appear spontaneously, but it is the product of skill and intensive effort. The anchors of the web are shown in Figure 4.1. Each will be discussed in detail. It is important, however, to remember that while each segment makes its own unique contribution, the full impact is the product of all the pieces. This is a case of the whole being greater than the sum of the parts.

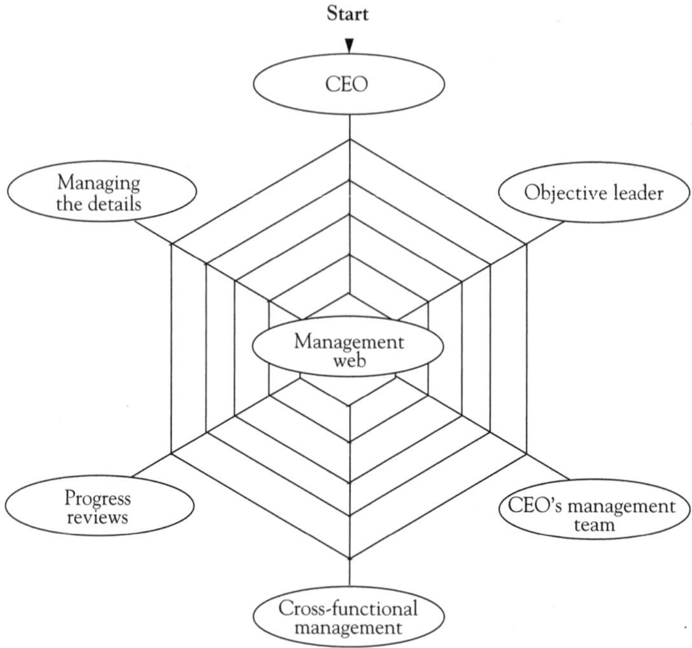

Figure 4.1: The management web and its anchors.

Every company has a framework within which business is conducted. In some cases this framework is driven by the personality of the CEO; in others it is the product of institutionalized systems. Regardless of the framework, there are some common threads: the framework is seldom documented and it seldom reflects the consensus of the top management team. This is because top management usually prefers to talk about the details of the business rather than about improving the framework for conducting the way business is done.

One of the critical elements that supports management by policy is an energetic senior management group which actually functions as a team. The CEO is the team leader. It is unlikely that this one person alone can determine the direction, explain the focus, and ensure that it is followed. All of this requires the dynamic assistance of a support team.

Role of the CEO

The CEO is responsible for ensuring that the systems are in place to guarantee the quality of products or services, that delivery is timely, that pricing is reasonable, that safe products are developed, and that community confidence is maintained. Each of these is required to ensure that a proper balance is provided in the pursuit of customer satisfaction and ultimately a profitable company.

This marks a subtle shift from the traditional ways of doing things. Usually each line organization was responsible for getting the job done. This usually took place within specified budget parameters and schedules that were based on past experience and available resources.

Now the CEO calls on the support team, which comprises the heads of those line organizations, to play a role that crosses functional lines. They now take on the dimension of helping the CEO ensure an optimum balance in meeting customer needs. In larger companies it just is not possible for the CEO to pay the kind of attention to detail that is necessary to ensure the optimum outcome.

For example, executives in charge of delivering products or services still will be responsible for the regular operations of their areas. They will also, however, take on the leadership role to ensure that all parties responsible for the quality of the products or services will be working together in the most effective way. Parties responsible include those who are not in the executive's line organization but are key players in ensuring product or service quality.

An example of this in the utility business requires the customer service staff to process requests from customers, then effectively interface with those who can initiate or restore electric service. This is particularly important when a company is organized in a manner that requires going to the top before a common cross-functional link is found. The organizational structure of cross-functional management comprises standing committees for each of the major cross-functional processes. Each committee is chaired by and comprised of senior executives to ensure that there is enough influence to overcome the resistance of the traditional organization's entrenched and vested interests. The purpose of each committee is to plan for and ensure the attainment of objectives through effective implementation of the means to accomplish these objectives. The committee ensures the *P* and the C of the PDCA cycle. The vertical/functional organization is accountable for the *D* and the *A* of the PDCA cycle. Figure 4.2 shows the interrelationships.

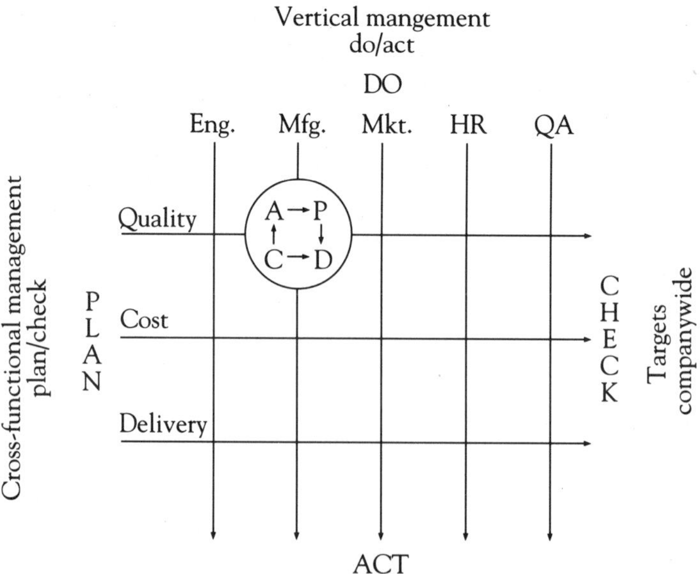

Source: *GOAL/QPC Research Report on Cross-Functional Management, Methuen, Mass.*

Figure 4.2: The interrelationships of various committees in the plan-do-check-act cycle.

The CEO meets regularly with each committee chairperson to review status. The cross-functional organization allows the CEO to manage the company horizontally as a series of processes instead of vertically by departments.

The CEO is a true team leader who never loses sight of the overall direction. At the same time the CEO uses the skills of coach, teacher, and expert in the field to optimize the impact of the team's efforts.

Role of the Objective Leader

Earlier the process for identifying areas for dramatic improvement was discussed. Now it is time to ensure that the improvement occurs. When a breakthrough or overarching objective for improvement is selected, it is very important that it is given a home. This means that a specific senior executive is designated as the one who will lead the effort to ensure successful achievement of that objective. This step can be disquieting to some senior executives. They might be uncertain as to why they have been chosen.

They will still be playing the old mental tapes that say, "This could fail. Your name will be associated with something that could fail." Senior executives know what can happen when their names are linked with failures. "I don't need this kind of visibility at this stage of my career," they think. "I'm being asked to do something and I don't even know what this something is." These are the thoughts of people who are more comfortable with the status quo than with being the standard bearers of change.

Another trap is that the improvement leader will be an ambitious grandstander who isn't a team player. Regardless, a senior executive is clearly put in charge. This is done to signify the importance of the challenge. In addition, it attacks head-on the tendency for something that is everyone's business to end up being nobody's business. The objective leader is the project manager. This person is ultimately accountable for the successful achievement of the project objective. The details of what an objective leader does are as follows:

1. Once the initial direction is established, the objective leader conducts an analysis to determine current performance in a manner that is quantifiable. The leader

considers the capability of existing processes to support desired performance and determines where the performance must be in the short term (one year) and in the long term (three to five years). This requires aggressive competitive analysis as well as patient benchmarking later in the process.

2. A leader must guide someone. The designation *project leader* connotes that more than one person's effort is required. It also suggests the need for stratification; that is, looking at various subsets of the task. Suppose the objective is to improve service to customers. Immediately analysis and stratification tell us that *improve service* applies to several areas, for example, locations one through seven and locations 11 through 15. In addition, it reveals that poor service is caused by inadequate checkout facilities at six locations, while it is caused by poor organization of materials at four other locations. This kind of stratification continues down to a level at which corrective action can be taken (see Figure 4.3).

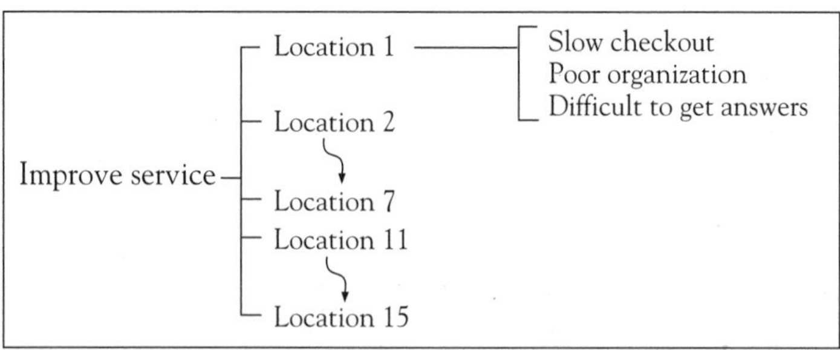

Figure 4.3: Problem stratification is a necessary prerequisite for appropriate corrective action.

The project leader is expected to be well informed on each step. Figure 4.4 shows an outline that will help keep track of the various pieces.

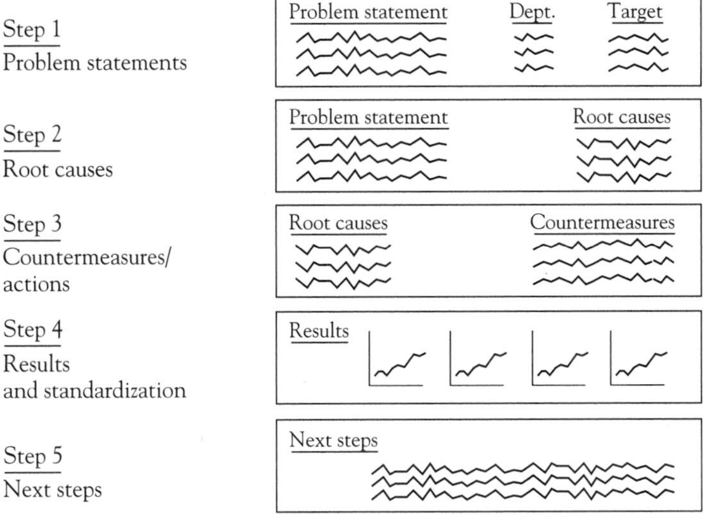

Figure 4.4: The objective leader's summary reporting format.

3. The objective leader crosses functional lines. This presents a challenge that is critical for success. Particularly in the early stages of the process, individuals in line organizations are easily threatened by what they perceive as interference from the outside. It is essential that one person has the authority to cut through the bureaucracy, which is all too often intent upon protecting its turf. When something is large enough to merit corporate attention for improvement it is unlikely that it is restricted to a single line organization. Therefore, clear leadership is required to ensure that focus is maintained.
4. People who can best contribute to the improvement are often reluctant to step forward. They might still see their involvement as something that will be added on to their regular work load. They might be uncomfortable with pursuing the analysis needed to develop the optimum response, or they might fear the consequences

of being unable to deliver everything that they had promised. It is the objective leader's responsibility to ensure that the analytical skills are in place and that the confidence is there to move forward.

5. The objective leader also acts as liaison with upper management, reporting what is attainable. This is the link back to the all-important cross-functional aspect of management at the top of the company.
6. Progress does not come by accident. The objective leader is the catalyst who ensures that the necessary steps are taken in a timely manner. Furthermore, the leader is the coach who encourages, teaches, lobbies for needed resources, gives feedback, and makes sure that the schedule is maintained.
7. The objective leader might also find that not enough is being done to meet the challenging targets. If so, the leader must take the initiative to muster further analysis, search out other processes that could benefit from improvement, and ensure that appropriate actions are taken to prevent a shortfall. This is a dynamic approach that requires constant attention and an aggressive response to all aspects of the endeavor.
8. The objective leader might conclude that, given other corporate constraints, the level of aggressiveness being sought is not appropriate. The role of mediator is the key to the success of the effort. It can be very difficult to explain to line managers that they cannot do as much as they wish to do once they are on board. The challenge is to be the consummate project manager.
9. The objective leader is expected not only to keep top management up to date on progress during the course of the year, but also to give a year-end report as well. This is somewhat different from conventional year-end reports. While attention is given to whether or not the target is met, there is also an expectation that the

process used to achieve the objective is itself under scrutiny. What worked? What didn't work? What could be improved for the next cycle? This attention to detail is easily lost in the conventional concern about whether or not targets are met.

In summary, the role of the objective leader is one of high visibility. This person must ensure that good intentions are not left to chance. The objective leader is the conscience of the corporation which strains to achieve dramatic improvement. The objective leader is a(n)

- Project manager
- Corporate analyst
- Broker of aggressive support
- Cross-functional liaison
- Link with senior management
- Reviewer of progress
- Initiator of interim adjustments
- Champion of those in difficult situations
- Keeper and enhancer of objective improvement process

Role of the CEO's Management Team

The choice of the word *team* is significant. We live in an age of superstars, in business, sports, and entertainment. There is a pattern that emerges time and time again when success is achieved. This pattern includes such elements as common vision, the ability to practice interdependence, the ability to understand the relationship between personal and group success, the ability to rise above personal idiosyncrasies and focus on a common mission, and skill in working through differences when conflicts arise.

The practical application of these concepts is often more visible in sports, but it is not exclusive to that field. It really doesn't matter how good a quarterback is if he gets sacked every time. It really doesn't matter how good the coach is if the offense, defense, and special teams don't produce.

Working with the team, the CEO must establish or confirm the corporate mission and vision. They develop company strategies based on objective analysis and assessment. They identify critical objectives for major corporate improvement. They monitor progress in achieving those improvement objectives. They allocate and manage resources in a manner that is consistent with the mission, vision, and major improvement objectives. They also constantly check to see that the infrastructure is in place to facilitate clear communication of their intentions and mirror their behavior.

It can be disconcerting for a senior management team to realize that their principles, practices, and behaviors quickly become the principles, practices, and behaviors of each succeeding level of the organization.

It is vital for top managers to understand that they must do the strategic planning. It must not be delegated to an external consulting firm or a corporate planning group. Data gathering and analysis can be provided by such sources, but only at top management's direction. It is not unusual for top managers to expect their planning groups to do all of the analysis and to make all of the recommendations from which top management makes the final selection. This must not happen! Instead, top managers must do the analysis and identify alternative recommendations.

Strategic planning by top managers is a core competency; it is critical to the success of the business. Without a top management team that does the strategic planning, the company's future cannot be guaranteed. The best execution in the world can't overcome bad strategy. World-class competitiveness demands both a world-class strategy and its world-class execution.

In summary, the CEO's management team

- Establishes and confirms the company's vision and mission
- Develops the company's strategies

- Targets critical objectives for major improvement
- Allocates resources consistent with vision, mission, and objectives
- Ensures implementation of the corporate infrastructure
- Monitors the corporate quality assurance system
- Periodically reviews and enhances the management system used to run the company

Cross-Functional Management

The term *cross-functional management* is very descriptive of how the process actually works. It literally means managing across functional boundaries. If this sounds like a revolutionary idea, it's because organizations tend to be territorial in nature. In most organizations there are frequent references to *my* department, *my* people, *my* equipment, or *my* product, as if individuals somehow owned them. This way of thinking is far removed from seeing oneself or one's co-workers as contributors to an overall process.

Cross-functional management has meaning at every level of an organization but is generally more critical the further up the organization we go. We have noted the importance of interdependence at the highest level of organizations. This interdependence needs to be rooted in the company's mission and vision.

We referred to the importance of establishing a clear mission and vision as a major responsibility of the CEO's management team. All of this is directly tied to the company's response to customer needs. This is what determines the true direction of the company. When interdependence is real and focused, then cross-functional management makes a lot of sense. It provides a structure that facilitates the nonthreatening crossing of functional lines. Different organizations will identify different areas for cross-functional attention.

Many companies that have implemented MBP have a permanent cross-functional committee for each of the following major areas that affect customer satisfaction.

- Product and service quality (quality assurance)
- Delivery (includes scheduling, cycle time reduction, and inventory reduction)
- Cost
- Safety
- Morale/social responsibility

The *quality* committee ensures product and service quality. Its main task is the continual improvement of an integrated quality assurance system for each department and for the major business processes including suppliers.

The aim of the *cost* committee is to ensure the right prices for customers and profits for the company. Cost targets are developed by subtracting profit from the selling price, which is market driven.

The *schedule* or *delivery* committee ensures that the right products and services are delivered at the right time and in the right quantities. It achieves increasing responsiveness and flexibility through supply-cycle time reduction.

Safety includes both product and employee safety and social/environmental protection and enhancement.

The *morale/social responsibility* committee typically is concerned with

- Employee development
- Employee involvement in improving the business
- Education and training
- New employee orientation
- Employee promotion
- Suggestion systems
- Reward/recognition
- Employee security
- The company's role as a key institution of society and trustee of its values

Figure 4.5 was adapted from a graphic developed by Ichiro Miyauchi in 1984. It shows the five elements of customer satisfaction. For each element there will be a standing cross-functional committee.

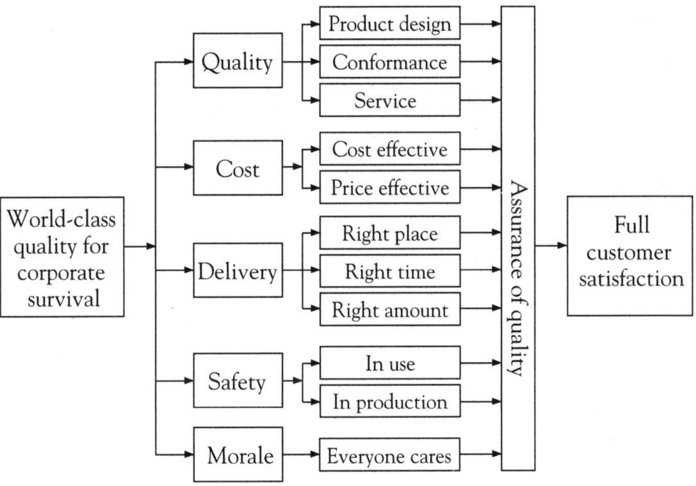

Adapted from Ichiro Miyauchi, *1984*.

Figure 4.5: The five elements of customer satisfaction. There should be a standing cross-functional team for each.

Because of the critical nature of new product or service development, many companies also have established a committee for new product development (NPD). Since the purpose of TQ is to satisfy the customer faster and better than does the competition, NPD is critical.

Each one of these areas is chaired by a member of the CEO's management team and in some cases by the CEO. For example, it is not unusual to see the CEO chair the new product development team because of its importance. There is an understanding that the chairpersons of these cross-functional committees represent the CEO. Members of the committees represent their functional areas.

With any of the five categories, it will probably be necessary to go across functional lines to ensure that customer needs are met. For example, a product's quality assurance is rarely found within one line organization. Raw materials are procured through the purchasing department and blueprints probably are drawn in the engineering department. The CEO's representative takes charge, pulls those people together, and leads them in establishing the process which will ensure the expected outcome. The CEO also supports them in establishing the measures that ensure that this process endures beyond the fleeting attention bestowed on it at one particular moment. What emerges is a dynamic approach to managing a business. The senior management team takes on the responsibility of satisfying the demands of product/service quality, delivery, cost, safety, and morale/social responsibility.

Product/service quality	Delivery	Cost	Safety	Morale/social responsibility

With a structure like this firmly in place at the top, it is much easier to implement an approach up and down the organizational ladder that recognizes the value of interdependence. If the department head is involved in cross-functional activities, sections within a department will find it difficult to protect their own turf at the expense of the rest of the department. In fact, one of the principal roles of a department head is to create the optimum environment for the individuals and specialists within that department to contribute as a member of a cross-functional team.

All of this involves a good news/bad news situation. The good news is that it does not require "Star Wars" technology to implement. The bad news is that it requires the understanding and implementation of an approach based on interdependence—something that is tedious, demanding, and anchored on sophisticated insights into human behavior. The following, more detailed, description of the cost committee further explains how cross-functional committees work.

The fundamental premise of the cross-functional cost committee is that cost is the result or outcome of various processes that comprise the company. Costs, therefore, will be reduced by improving processes. For example, Toyota's vaunted production system, also called the just-in-time system, is geared to eliminate all waste from the production process. Toyota's system has the following characteristics: level schedules; extremely short set-up times (less than ten minutes); parts-per-million defect rates; flexible workers and processes; standardized, cellular processes; small group improvement activities; visual controls; and a pull system of scheduling whereby parts are produced only if the customer operation sends a signal.

Developing such a system reduces costs. It is important to add that inventory reduction is viewed as both a result of process improvement and a means to accomplish process improvement. Inventory reduction is a means because inventory masks problems. Often extra inventory is maintained to compensate for unreliable equipment and quality problems. By purposely reducing inventory by an arbitrary degree, the contingency is removed and problems become visible. Considered in this way, inventory reduction is a means to accomplish process improvement, which translates into cost reduction.

The cost committee is responsible for developing policies for the attainment of cost and profit objectives and for the periodic review that compares actual performance to the plan. At Toyota, the cost committee is supported by the following full-time sections in the cost management department.

1. Cost *planning,* which is a resource for the development of cost targets for new products
2. Cost *control,* which develops profit plans and budgets and is responsible for cost and financial accounting
3. Cost *improvement,* which promotes the improvement of costs in production

The cross-functional cost committee has final approval for price, profit, and cost plans for long-term, intermediate, and annual plans and for specific new products and product changes.

The Japanese cost management is based upon a system of target costs. The system starts with a determination of product selling prices based upon customer expectations. The target profit is then subtracted to determine the target costs. They maintain standard costs to verify profit attainment and routinely recalculate standard costs once or twice a year. There is, however, no periodic determination or analysis of the variance between standard costs and actual costs.

For new products, target costs are developed for every part in the product, considering experience and extrapolation of improvement efforts. The target-setting effort is coordinated by the cost planning section with a high degree of input from engineering and purchasing. Target costs are included on all part drawings.

Engineering then designs to obtain the target through the incorporation of new technology and the application of value engineering and robust design approaches. Although it originated in the west, value engineering is another concept that has been used much more extensively by the Japanese. The robust design process uses designed experiments to identify the optimum values of important design factors. It starts by using the lowest-cost materials. Only if necessary will more expensive materials be used to achieve the intent of the design. In this way, designers ensure that the lowest-cost materials are used. Since materials typically account for the majority of total costs (60 to 80 percent), this guarantees the lowest-cost design. Various sources at Toyota feel that during the past decade approximately 80 percent of all their improvements, including cost reduction, were accomplished through value engineering and robust design. Reduction of overhead costs such as energy is also targeted. Cost reduction targets are apportioned to each major department, organization level by organization level. Also, all individuals are encouraged to identify cost reduction ideas and to submit them through the suggestion system. Targeted percentage reductions vary by department and by level within each department depending upon an analysis of what is appropriate. A single cost reduction percentage is not mandated for all departments. Direct labor is considered a period cost. Cost target deployment is coordinated and reviewed regularly by the cross-functional cost committee.

As mentioned previously, cost reduction and delivery attainment improvements are outcomes of process improvements. Since lasting process improvements depend upon a quality assurance system, good cost management and delivery management depend upon quality assurance. Therefore, the quality committee is viewed as the cornerstone committee of the entire cross-functional structure.

We have discussed how each cross-functional committee deploys policies vertically, level by level, in each department. It is also important to emphasize that each committee deploys policies horizontally. In practice, the committees are highly integrated. Since the same top managers are members of the various cross-functional committees, the integration of all committee efforts is greatly facilitated. Traditionally, companies have addressed quality, cost, and schedules separately, each as a unique equation to be solved independently. The excellent Japanese companies address all concurrently, more like solving a set of simultaneous equations.

Progress Reviews

Progress reviews are another critical element in the management web. It is important to start with the distinction between constructive and destructive reviews. A destructive review is one where the reviewer uses the opportunity to vent frustration, play out personal agendas, exercise inappropriate power of position, or otherwise treat the person being reviewed in a manner that is demeaning or disrespectful. A constructive review is one where the reviewer follows a path of diagnosis, accurately determining the current status of progress and identifying the gaps and weaknesses, leading to feedback that provides a basis for action and that can be tied to a schedule.

This distinction is critical to understanding the review process. It can be the difference between success and failure. Good feedback is at the heart of reviews. It is important to realize that this tool existed long before management by policy. In this discussion we will talk about four different kinds of reviews. All are closely linked and actually serve as building blocks leading from one to another.

Level I Review

This review (see Figure 4.6a) is usually conducted by those who report to the CEO. Working with the CEO, they have determined the company's direction and the key strategies. They have approved the annual plan including the resources necessary to support it. Now it is essential that they follow up. While there is no magic number for the frequency of these reviews, it seems that the following schedule might support the smooth flow of the annual business cycle.

Progress reviews			
Level	Frequency	Reviewer	Reviewee
I	3/year	Senior executives	Department heads
II			
III			

Figure 4.6a: Level I progress review.

For those whose business year begins on January 1, the first progress review is very beneficial during the month of January. This gives an opportunity to make a final review of the previous year's business, to assess the lessons learned, to determine that the new plan is understood, to ensure that analysis has been done, and to ensure that the implementation of proposed countermeasures is clearly mapped out. It sends a very strong signal that top management is prepared, that it understands how the priorities have been derived, and that it is aware that there is a clear agenda for that year.

A second review is held in the May–June time frame. This allows for reasonable progress in the implementation of countermeasures for the current year, and it provides the opportunity to start things rolling for the following year. In an environment where planning drives budgeting, it is important to determine next year's priorities.

A third review is held in November. At this stage it is easy to project year-end status. If the countermeasures have not proved as successful as originally anticipated, it is not too late to make additional efforts to achieve the desired results. This is also an appropriate time to assess the completeness of the planning and budgeting preparation for the following year.

Level II Review

The level II progress review (see Figure 4.6b) is normally conducted by department heads. Those reviewed are usually the ones who report directly to the department heads. The review focuses on company priorities, the department's link to those priorities, and on other business objectives that are key to the department's success. These reviews might be conducted as often as once each quarter. At this level issues of prioritization will be discussed, as will particular analyses and selected countermeasures. Progress on the actual implementation of the countermeasures as well as results already achieved will be discussed.

Progress reviews			
Level	Frequency	Reviewer	Reviewee
I	3/year	Senior executives	Department heads
II	4/year	Department heads	Middle managers
III			

Figure 4.6b: Levels I and II progress reviews.

Level III Review

The third level of review (see Figure 4.6c) facilitates a structured interaction between middle managers and their direct reports. The focus continues to be on corporate priorities and on the other important things done at that level. It must be realized that some of the critical things done at the supervisor's level might not be tied directly to the few corporate priorities because the business of the company is more extensive than those carefully selected priorities.

Here the reviews can get quite detailed. This is the level at which specific problems are identified, analysis is conducted, and countermeasures are implemented. The ability to connect these activities back to the corporate priorities is one of the elements that makes this approach different from others.

Progress reviews			
Level	Frequency	Reviewer	Reviewee
I	3/year	Senior executives	Department heads
II	4/year	Department heads	Middle managers
III	Monthly	Middle managers	Supervisors/others

Figure 4.6c: Levels I, II, and III progress reviews.

This discussion on reviews has been conducted from the perspective of a large enterprise. Adjustments must be made to best suit every company. For example, if there are few employees and one layer of management, then there is just the one level of review. The key is to understand why a review is needed and then proceed in a manner that is flexible and appropriate.

CEO Review

The kinds of progress reviews discussed thus far represent a look at progress from a vertical or departmental/functional perspective. But you might remember this question from earlier discussions: how many of the areas targeted for major corporate improvement require the kind of support that cuts across those functional lines?

The CEO audit (called the presidential audit in Japan) is an effective tool for supporting the kind of cross-functional effort required (see Figure 4.6d). The approach is simple. The areas targeted for major corporate attention are managed by an objective leader. Once each month the CEO selects one of the major areas

Progress reviews			
Level	Frequency	Reviewer	Reviewee
I	3/year	Senior executives	Department heads
II	4/year	Department heads	Middle managers
III	Monthly	Middle managers	Supervisors/others
CEO	Monthly	CEO/other top executives	Objective leaders and other selected presenters

Figure 4.6d: The role of the CEO audit along with levels I, II, and III audits.

for detailed attention. Some or all of the CEO's immediate team participate in the review. Working through the items will probably take most of a day.

The session will start with an overview of why this particular area was chosen for major corporate attention. An explanation is provided on how the target for improvement was developed and whether or not it is a valid target. A description is given of the corporate-level analysis that was completed. The capability of the processes related to the improvements is discussed. A clear summary of how the problem area is stratified is shared and a summary of progress to date is given. This portion can be concluded with a description of the system that has been developed to ensure that the spirit of continuous improvement has been preserved throughout the effort.

A logical follow-up to the presentations is the sharing of some specific improvements that have been identified and developed. These usually will be representative of cross-functional activities. They will also include examples of areas where significant progress is made, as well as areas of difficulty. It is critical to understand that this pursuit is positive and aggressive.

The purpose is to demonstrate that this is important at every level of the organization. It is examined in such great detail to ensure that barriers are eliminated and that resources are optimized in the pursuit of something that is critical to the health of the company.

By way of summary, a listing of all countermeasures now being implemented can be shared along with a brief progress report. At the end of the session it is appropriate to recap any actions that might have been recommended. The CEO should thank the presenters for their progress as well as for their efforts in responding to questions during the session. Once the session is adjourned, it is appropriate for the CEO and the rest of the team to spend some time assessing the strengths and weaknesses of what they had observed. In addition, they must develop recommendations and determine when they would like to follow up on this particular improvement objective. The unique challenge in this review is for the CEO and the team to function in a diagnostic role rather than in the role of answer suppliers.

This comprehensive approach to reviews is a powerful tool. Like so many powerful tools, however, it can be destructive when used without benefit of mature understanding.

First, the reviewers must focus on the business of the company—the hard challenges facing the company and the individual departments. Second, those who are accountable for the contributions are reviewed. The development of a cadre of professional presenters must be avoided. Third, the skills required to conduct effective reviews must be studied and practiced with great diligence. Otherwise, the process becomes an exercise in demotivation, confusion, and backsliding.

Progress Reviews—What Is Different?

The first thing that is different is the expectation that progress is monitored with great interest every step of the way. This is done from the perspective of continuous improvement and with a view to ensuring success at the end of the effort rather than just hoping that things will turn out well.

Second, there is a clear focus on what is critical to the success of the company. This has been determined from the customer's perspective.

Third, the efforts to ensure this success are not left to chance. They are the product of comprehensive analysis, project management, and attention to detail.

Fourth, comprehensive analysis creates the potential for getting to the actual causes of the problem. The reviews encourage this approach and reinforce the practice. This greatly increases the probability that the correct countermeasures or solutions are identified and implemented.

Fifth, the built-in alignment that the review structure encourages does wonders for keeping the focus on the customer, reducing duplication of effort, limiting non–value-added activities, and simplifying work processes. The ability of an organization to accomplish this on an ongoing basis is far more dramatic than current practices, which are akin to spring cleaning, where once in a while someone comes in with lots of fanfare and cleans house.

Sixth, there is an expectation of continuous improvement rather than mere reporting on the current situation. This is fundamental to empowerment because it moves the perspective from hand-wringing about the present to that of gaining control over what causes the present situation and to improving it for the future.

Finally, it focuses attention on the work processes themselves. It deals with questions such as "What are the processes?" "What is the performance of those processes?" "Can outcomes be predicted based on upstream performance?" "Are the processes capable of delivering what is expected?" This is a refreshing, powerful, and workable approach as contrasted with the practice of seeking out someone to blame. The spirit of the review must be to better understand the processes involved, rather than to blame individuals for bad results.

Managing the Details

The theory of management by policy makes a lot of sense, but, to those who see themselves as big-picture people, it can cause a certain annoyance. They argue that for the most part "this is just common sense" and "something we have always known." "It is not that different," they claim. The most dramatic difference is frequently seen in the management of details. Without clear problem identification, root cause analysis, and effective implementation of countermeasures, all driven by the need to satisfy customers, the approach would be much the same. Without meticulous follow-through and the creation of systems that eliminate the need to solve the same problem again and again, there is little to add. Management by policy requires persistence and, above all, stretches management skill in walking the fine line between broad perspective and attention to detail.

The objective leader must ensure that critical components are clearly in place. These include the identification of the corporate-level problem, stratification into its component parts throughout the organization, identification of those who can participate in the solution, and determination of process capability and potential contribution to improvement. All are supported by the structure of reviews.

The following is a case study that captures some of the attention to detail necessary for success. It begins with input from the customer stating that customer service, particularly in the area of billing accuracy, is unacceptable. Furthermore, it is said to be dramatically worse than the competition. The case study is presented from the point of view of an executive who is following up to ensure that the objective is being pursued in a manner that will ensure long-term success. Figure 4.7 shows the kind of information that the executive expects to see.

At the local or specific improvement level, project management skills play a major role. Clearly identifying who, what, when, where, why, and how ensures a solid infrastructure that facilitates progress (see Figure 4.8). This level of attention makes it easy to pursue the level of detail required to ensure that targets are met.

There are many good project management tools on the market. The choice is best driven by practicality. More important than using the best software is understanding how this tool is used. First, it helps the objective leader track the many improvement contributions. Second, it makes the actions and schedules visible. Third,

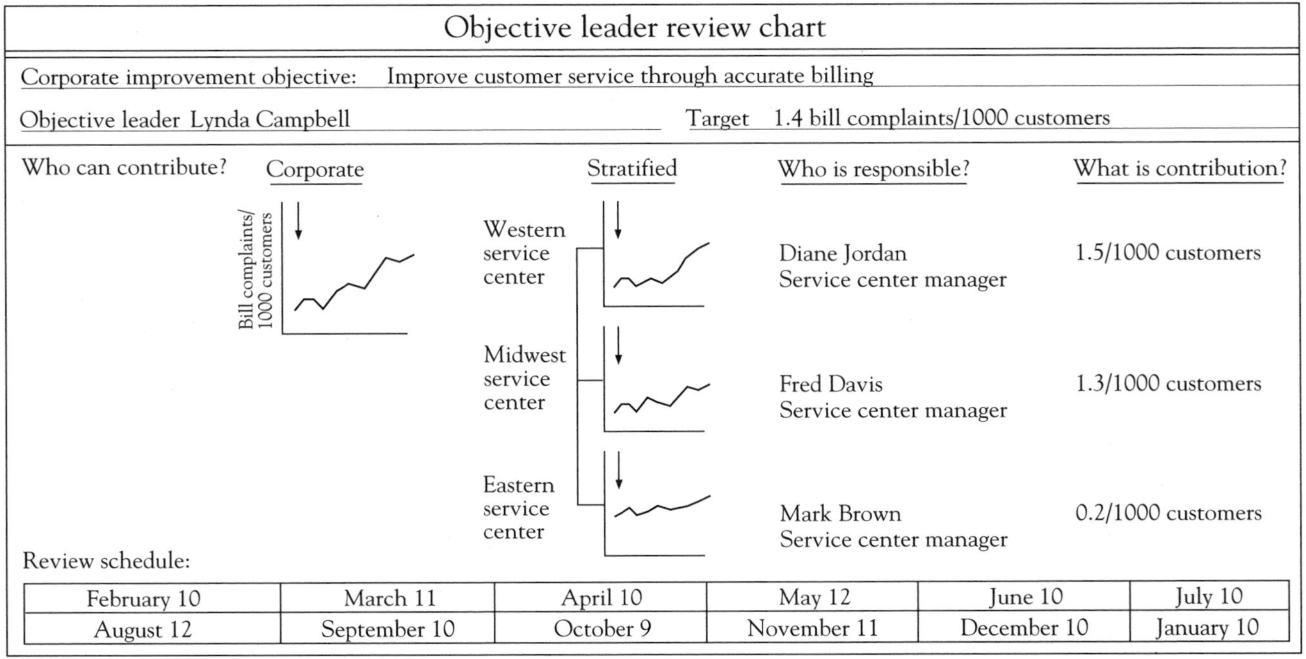

February 10	March 11	April 10	May 12	June 10	July 10
August 12	September 10	October 9	November 11	December 10	January 10

Figure 4.7: Objective leader review chart.

REVIEWEE: Diane Jordan LOCATION: Western Service Center DATE: December 10

Improvement objective:

- Corporate: Improve customer service through accurate billing — Target: 1.4/1000 customers
- Local: Reduce number of incorrect bills sent to customers — Target: 1.5/1000 customers

#	Problem	Actions taken	Who is responsible?	Implementation schedule												Comments
				J	F	M	A	M	J	J	A	S	O	N	D	
1.	Missing information	a) Develop checklist for clerks	Rick Ward	→												Checklist completed before processing
		b) Enhance computer software	Rick Ward	→	→	→	→	→	→	→	→	→	→	→	→	
2.	Incorrect amounts charged	a) Simplify price codes	Marvin Wilson	→	→	→	→	→	→	→	→	→				
		b) Standardize and update price list monthly	Marvin Wilson	→	→	→	→	→	→	→	→	→	→	→	→	All sales reps to receive list by 5th of month
		c) Training on new price structure	Marvin Wilson	→	→	→										All employees trained on new price structure
3.	Charges for service/items not included	a) Cross-training with sales reps	Rick Ward	→	→	→	→	→								To be done with sales reps in the field
		b) Review/redesign interoffice billing request form	Team	→	→	→	→	→	→	→						Reformat
		c) Eliminate outdated pricing structures	Rick Ward	→	→	→	→									Review all procedures to assure relevance

Figure 4.8: Local review chart.

it clearly identifies those responsible for actions. Finally, it serves as a simple tracking document that provides a common framework for everyone involved.

Since feedback is at the heart of continuous improvement, it is reasonable to expect that the project management activity itself is supported by this very effective tool. In the course of a good review, several insights will occur and additional opportunities for action will be identified. It is critical that these are captured in a manner that ensures further action. This is easily done in a review follow-up document (see Figure 4.9).

This document will reflect basic summary information including reference to results achieved with brief comparisons between plans and actual accomplishments. Furthermore, it can capture general observations such as progress to date, recommendations on tools and alternatives, and even some motivational comments. Homework, too, might result from this process. It is not left to chance. Rather, it is captured and immediately becomes part of a follow-up system. Note that the worksheet in Figure 4.9 is specific, concrete, and focused.

This approach to implementing MBP—including the attention to detail as discussed—assumes discipline, project management skills, cross-functional cooperation, focus on customer needs, focus on process, and an instinct for success. Without this instinct for success the need for attention to details will probably be difficult to maintain.

MBP and Daily Management

Some companies view the overall company management system as comprising three subsystems—management by policy (MBP), cross-functional management (CFM), and daily management (DM). These subsystems are integrated and highly interdependent.

Daily management is the foundation for cross-functional management and MBP. It is a system by which everyone in the company performs their work on a daily basis in a manner that is reliable and consistent.

REVIEWEE: Diane Jordan LOCATION: Western Service Center DATE: February 10

Improvement objective:

- Corporate: Improve customer service through accurate billing — Target: 1.4/1000 customers
- Local: Reduce number of incorrect bills sent to customers — Target: 1.5/1000 customers

Problem	Analysis	Actions taken	Results	Contribution	
				Plan	Actual
1. Missing information	15% of incorrect bills related to missing info	a) Checklist for clerks b) Enhanced computer software	a) Completed 1/10 b) No progress to date	0.07	0.04
2. Incorrect amounts charged	19% of incorrect bills related to incorrect amounts charged	a) Simplify pricing codes b) Standardize/update price list monthly c) Train on new price structure	a) Completed 1/10 b) Incomplete c) Completed 1/10	0.12	0.10
3. Charges for services not included	60% of incorrect billls related to missing charges	a) Cross-training/sales b) Review/redesign interoffice form c) Eliminate outdated structures	a) Incomplete b) Team assigned c) Completed 1/20	0.31	0.27

General observations:

- Good communication and deployment
- Good stratification of problem areas
- Actions not adequate to achieve target

Homework:

What?	Who?	When?
a) Develop action plan to enhance software	Rick Ward	3/11
b) Complete standardization of price list	Marvin Wilson	3/11
c) Continue analysis to assure that targets are met	Diane Jordan	Ongoing
d) Schedule cross-training	Rick Ward	3/11

Figure 4.9: Local review record.

As a system, DM is organized around processes that are specifically related to a major functional area, such as production. The scope of DM activities includes both the maintenance and incremental improvement of current process standards. Elements of this system include the following:

1. Process descriptions in terms of flowcharts
2. QC process charts, control points for process outcomes, and check points for process control parameters
3. Operation standards
4. Descriptions of roles, responsibilities, and accountabilities
5. Data requirements (type, collection method and frequency, and reporting method and frequency)
6. Procedures for maintenance
7. Procedures for corrective action when special causes occur
8. Procedures for daily improvement
9. Procedures for the suggestion system
10. Methods for intradepartmental and intraprocess coordination
11. Procedures for employee recognition

DM is used as the basis for

1. Maintaining awareness of the current level of performance
2. Determining breakthrough areas for MBP
3. Determining improvement priorities.
4. Planning—annual, midterm, and long range

An example of determining breakthrough areas for MBP is as follows. As a result of daily improvement activities, a certain incremental rate of improvement, say 10 percent, is expected throughout the coming year on a given process. An analysis of customer needs by management determines that the process must be improved by

30 percent. The difference between 10 and 30 percent represents an area where breakthrough is required, as shown in Figure 4.10.

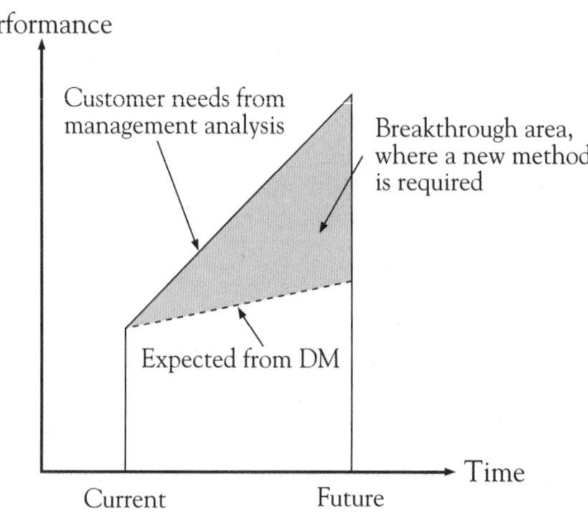

Source: Deltapoint

Figure 4.10: How to determine a breakthrough area for management by policy.

Determining improvement priorities is done as follows. For each basic work unit a priority list is developed that integrates maintenance, DM improvement, cross-functional management committee improvement, and breakthrough activities.

Daily management provides MBP with the current organizational status, including process capabilities and chronic problems. It also is the means by which gains from breakthrough achievements are maintained and standardized throughout the organization as shown in Figure 4.11.

This is done by using the standardize-do-check-act cycle (SDCA)—a modification of the PDCA cycle—specifically for process standardization. Control items from the MBP system are integrated into DM for daily control.

Noriaki Kano uses the analogy of an ocean liner to explain the relationship between DM, MBP, and cross-functional management

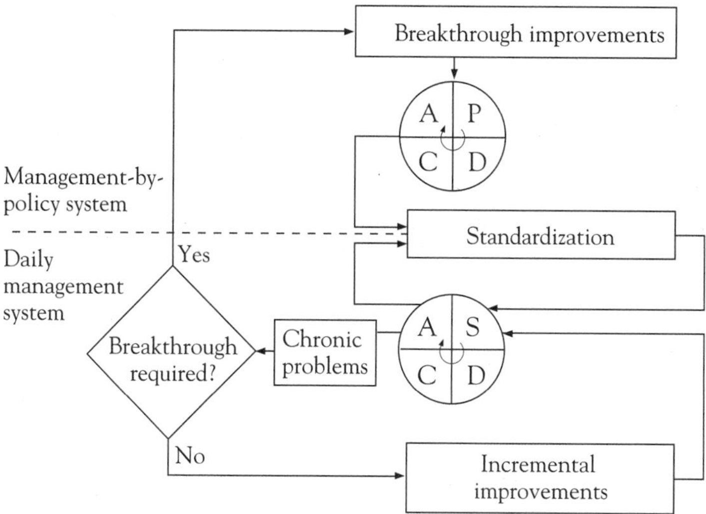

Source: Modification of a chart by Amon, Collins, Dmytrow, and Ward from "QIP: FPL's Continuous Improvement Process," 1989 ASQC Annual Quality Congress Proceedings

Figure 4.11: The relationship between MBP and DM.

(see Figure 4.12). MBP determines and sets the ship's course, especially changes in direction. DM maintains the direction by keeping the ship operationally functional.

Cross-functional management provides the structure which ensures that horizontal cross-functional processes dominate the traditional vertical hierarchical organization. Within a department, cross-functional activities are given priority over activities that relate only to that department. Having senior executives as the members of cross-functional committees ensures that cross-functional priorities are executed. These committees typically meet monthly to compare progress to the plan. Where there are gaps between actual results and the plan, the committees determine the root causes. Since most MBP policies are cross-functional, the cross-functional organization is the means by which these MBP policies are deployed and reviewed.

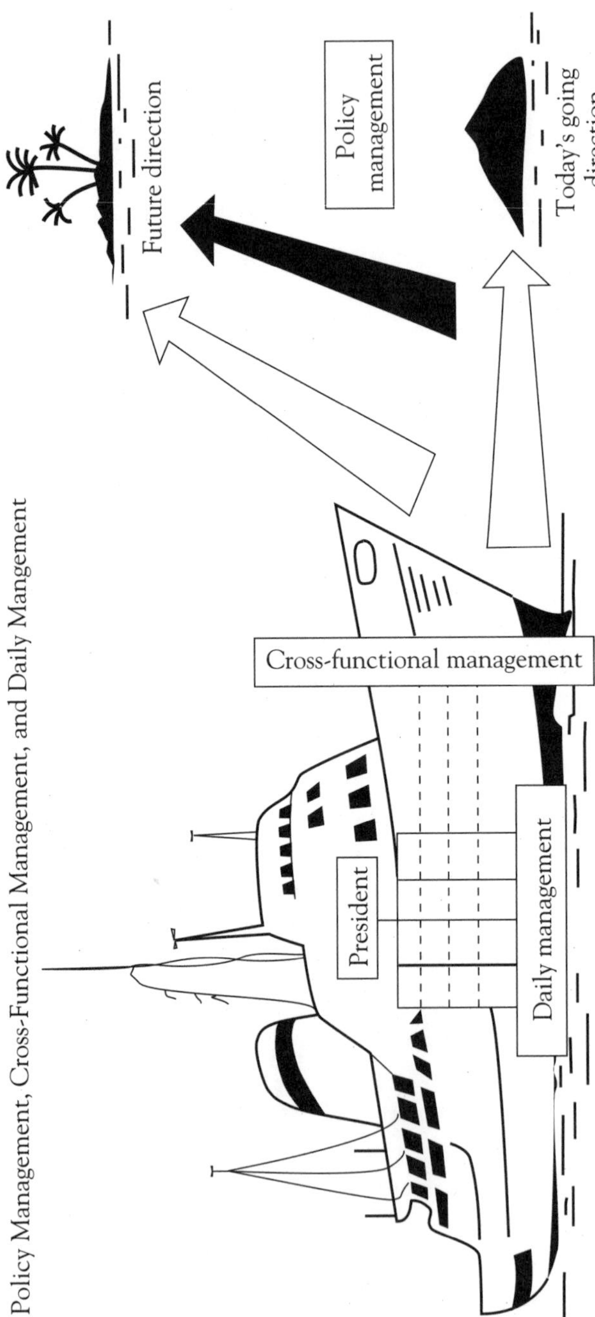

© *Noriaki Kano, 1987 JUL*

Figure 4.12: Management by policy changes the ship's direction.

As stated previously, there is a cross-functional committee for each of the five major categories of customer satisfaction—product and/or service quality, cost, delivery, safety, and morale/social responsibility. A number of companies also have a new product development (NPD) committee. Each committee coordinates the planning and execution of policies within departments and appoints ad hoc committees to address key subprocesses that are cross-functional.

For example, the NPD committee might appoint a team to analyze the engineering change process, which is a subset of the total NPD process, but cross-functional nonetheless. Figure 4.13 shows how the three management subsystems—MBP, CFM, and DM relate to total quality principles and to business results. The three management systems provide the structure by which the TQ principles are applied to ensure customer satisfaction and thereby the achievement of world-class competitiveness.

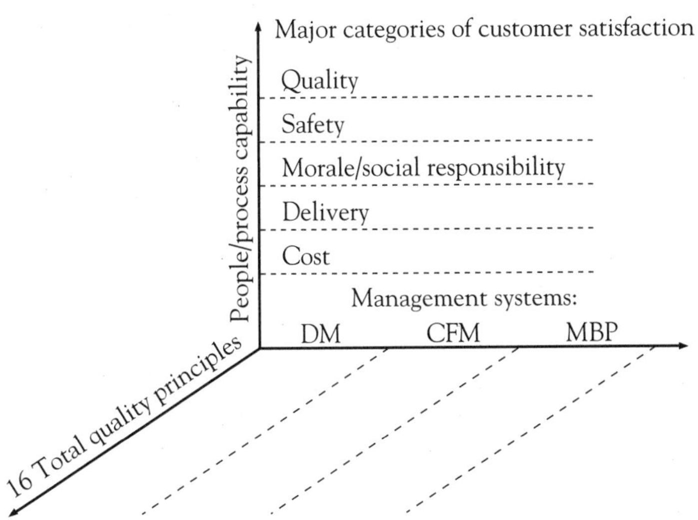

Figure 4.13: Management by policy, cross-functional management, and daily management ensure that total quality principles are applied to attain business results.

Organizational complexity often obscures the relationship between what the customer requires and what the line departments actually do. The first step requires establishing a clear link between those requirements and what is actually done deep inside the company. Once departments realize that their actions are in direct support of the customer—though sometimes somewhat removed—they will be more willing to improve. This direct link and the clear focus have a much more powerful impact than mere exhortation to do better. Improvements can often be made at the local level; this is day-to-day application of continuous improvement. But there are times when more is needed. The desired improvement might extend beyond the neat boundaries of the conventional department, might be critical and urgent, or the process itself might actually need radical restructuring to ensure optimum performance. Given any or all of these circumstances, management by policy will be necessary to accomplish the level of changes required.

What Makes Management by Policy Different? —Lessons Learned

1. *Ability to prioritize*. When we're faced with many issues that are both urgent and critical, it can be difficult to avoid the trap of trying to do everything at once. The discipline of management by policy forces a company to cast a cold eye on what is going on and, from the customer's perspective, prioritize those things that are most critical for success. The ability to select the vital few is central to the achievement of dramatic improvement. Without it, the analysis and coordination required for this kind of effort can be overwhelming.
2. *Catchball is vital*. It matters little what this process is called, but the reality is that there is no substitute for the interaction required as stratification and analysis

are pursued throughout the organization. The tendency to grab at quick fixes or to ramrod expert solutions is always inviting. It is also divisive and rarely results in ownership. This issue is further complicated by the common perception that there is little room for the use of soft skills, particularly in an environment that requires dramatic changes.

3. *The actions must add up*. Merely setting a target is not enough. First, it must be the correct target, consistent with process capabilities. Second, analysis is required to determine the root cause of the gap between current performance and the target. Only then is it possible to select the actions that ensure that this gap is closed. This can be tedious and demanding, but the outcome is that the gap is closed—and it stays closed.
4. *Clear leadership*. This does not happen by accident. It requires a designated project manager at the executive level. Given that it is so important to the company, it should be worthy of executives' attention. The executives must be comfortable with both the tenets of TQ and the tools of project management.
5. *Use of basic and new tools*. The discussion of management by policy often reverts to analysis, which is at the heart of the process and, of course, is dependent on the proper selection of analytical tools. For the most part those are the seven basic QC tools—cause-and-effect diagrams, check sheets, control charts, histograms, line graphs, Pareto charts, and scatter diagrams—as well as selected new tools such as the affinity, relation, and tree diagrams. The remaining new tools are an integral part of the project management process. Overall, a blend of patience and discipline is the vital ingredient that must be perfected to ensure the effective implementation of management by policy.

Summing up Management by Policy—An Integrated Approach

When a company embarks on management by policy it is important that the question "Why?" be asked as frequently as "What?" The question "What?" merely outlines the steps and these alone only provide a structure. The question "Why?" provides the meaning behind the structure. It is this understanding that will ensure permanence and depth of implementation.

The flowchart in Figure 4.14 can greatly enhance insight into relationships between key players and critical activities. Senior executives are key players in each of the three phases of management by policy. Their role in establishing, deploying, and implementing goes far beyond providing a stamp of approval; it goes to the heart of managing the business in a manner that is proactive and data driven and that reflects consensus. Once the players and the steps are established and there is a comfort level with the question "Why?" then it is merely a matter of working out the details. Of course, the details can cause little turf skirmishes. For example, who is responsible for establishing customer needs? This question is about how to provide staff support for senior executives; it should not be confused with the actual development of direction and management of the company.

How all of this happens is the key to ongoing success. The concept of catchball has been discussed in detail; its spirit must permeate the total effort. This is not something unique; it is the essence of good communication built on common courtesy and a realization that none of us likes to have things stuffed down our throats. Buy-in rates right up there along with logic and intellectual understanding. For MBP to work they must exist side by side.

Reviews, too, are central to good communication. They have to do with expectations, interest, willingness to help when things are difficult, continued focus on priorities, and an overall sense of urgency. When these aspects of communication fail, the reviews take on a different tone, but this is a failure in execution rather than a failure of the concept.

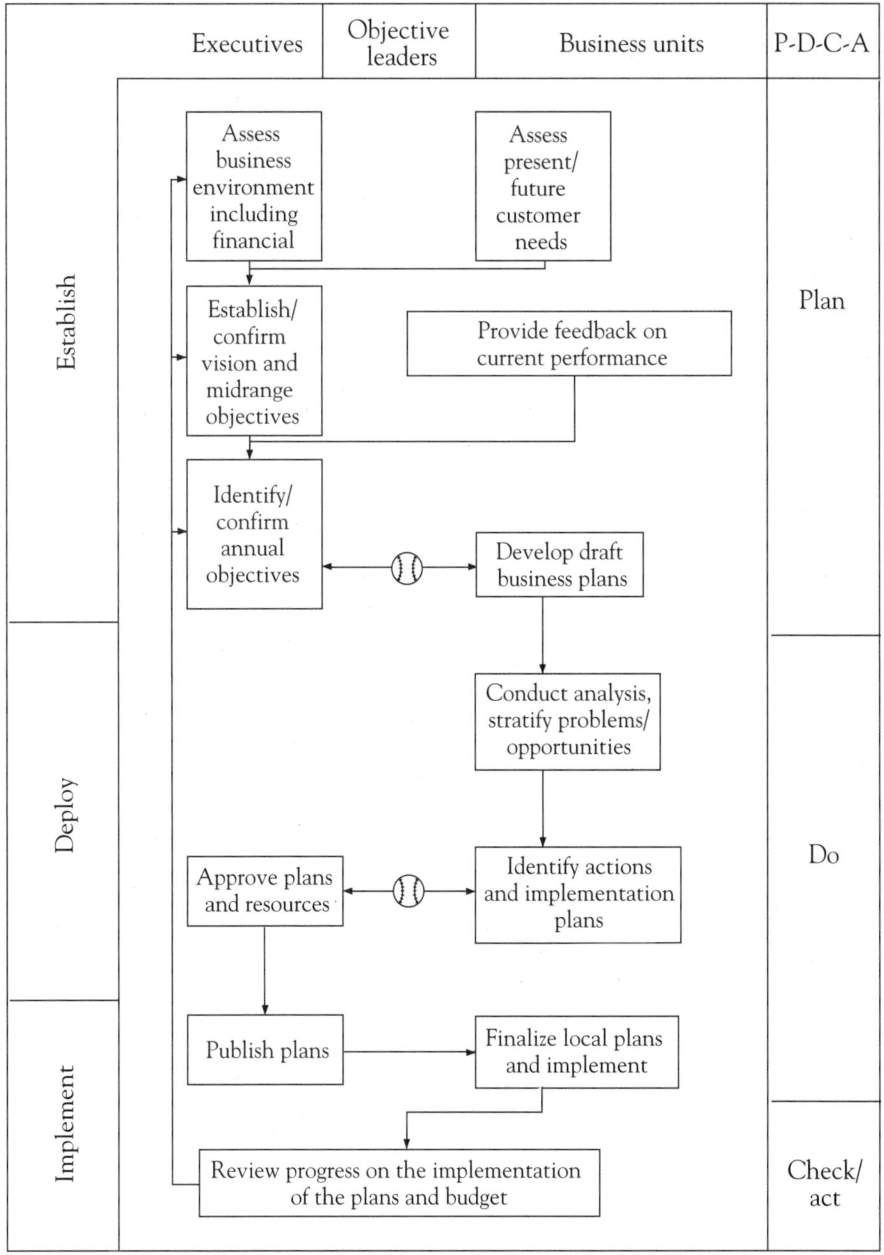

Figure 4.14: Management by policy: an integrated approach.

The integrated approach must make sense in the environment in which it is proposed. It is not a model imposed from the outside, but an integral framework that can be used to structure challenges and change. It is a dynamic framework that is driven by the basic principles of management by policy.

Each step is deliberate and builds on the principles of TQ. It starts with the identification of the objective leader. This selection is premised on who can have the most impact, or, more basic still, who is the absolutely best choice. Contrast this with the who-can-we-spare? approach.

Target selection, likewise, seems like an innocuous term. But behind this are a myriad of assumptions that reflect such aspects as process capability, benchmarking, and, above all, customer requirements.

The who-can-contribute? approach can be very misleading. It is nothing more than a succinct summary of a series of analytical steps which result in an action plan. It sums up a systematic approach beginning with comprehensive analysis at the corporate process level. It then follows a path that is consistent with Pareto analysis, leading to specific areas requiring detailed cause-and-effect analysis. Ultimately, actions are identified which, when effectively implemented, bring about the desired improvement. The review schedule section might also appear obvious and even smack of an overstructured approach. The reality is that completing this simple schedule requires a sound understanding of project management and the need for cross-functional attention when major corporate improvements are attempted.

Overall, what is at stake is the difference between casual improvement and dramatic systematic change. This can easily equate to the difference between success and failure.

Note how the flow diagram of an integrated approach to management by policy relates to the PDCA cycle. It builds from one year to the next. Management by policy is the way that advanced TQ companies turn the PDCA wheel on the task of providing breakthrough competitive advantage.

5

Implementing a Management-by-Policy System

Total quality does not guarantee the companies will produce strategies. Winning strategies must come from the minds of the leaders, augmented by input from the troops.

—Edwin Artzt
Chairman & CEO, Procter & Gamble

Introduction

We've explained management by policy as practiced by Deming Prize-winning companies—MBP's most advanced degree. There are some variations in the application of MBP principles among these companies, such as starting the policy development process from the middle of the organization instead of from the top. All of the elements we've described, however, are present. Attaining the degree of competency we have described will take a number of years, even for some companies that are well along in their total quality journey. What are the best ways to implement MBP? What are the prerequisites, implementation principles, and pitfalls? The purpose of this chapter is to provide guidance for implementing an MBP system.

Approaches to Implementation

The classical way to implement MBP is to do things in the following sequence. First, have a critical mass of competency throughout the organization using the PDCA cycle to improve processes and the SDCA cycle to maintain and standardize improvements. Get most of the critical processes in control and capable. Have at least 50 to 60 percent of all persons involved in formal process improvement teams. In short, put the daily management system in place. Second, proactively assess customers' needs and have a reliable method for translating needs into product and/or service requirements. Develop a prevention-based approach for critical cross-functional business systems. In essence, this step involves implementing a cross-functional management system.

Third, implement management by policy. Although there is significant overlap in these three steps, generally this sequence is followed as shown in Figure 5.1.

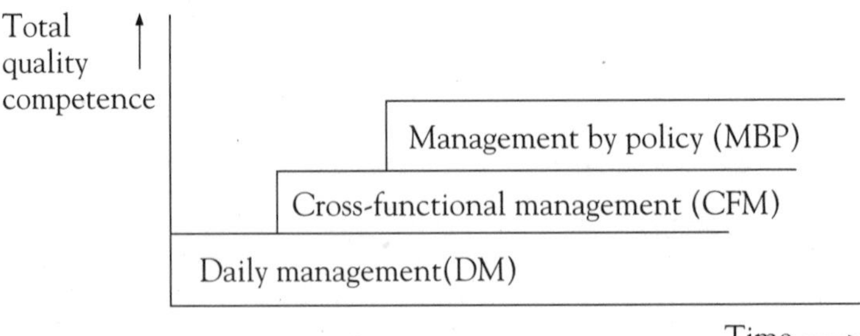

Figure 5.1: The management-by-policy implementation sequence.

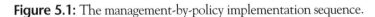

Referring to the general model for TQ implementation presented in chapter 2, Figure 5.2 shows how the previous sequence overlays onto this general five-phase model.

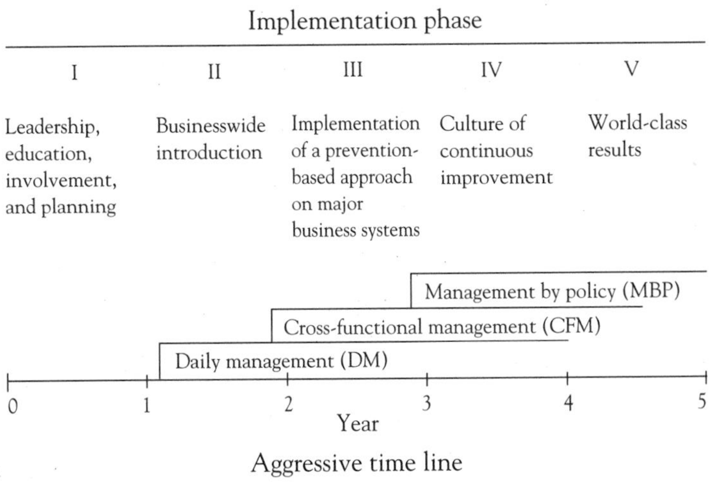

Figure 5.2: How the MBP sequence fits into the model for TQ implementation.

Juki, a sewing machine manufacturer, system provider, and a Deming Prize winner, compares the implementation of *hoshin kanri* or MBP to building a house in four steps. In the first step individuals develop a capability to solve their problems. The second, third, and fourth steps are analogous to DM, CFM, and MBP. Figure 5.3 shows the graphic that Juki uses to describe implementation.

Most U.S. companies that are implementing MBP generally follow the classical sequence, although they are taking longer than the aggressive timetable that we've shown. Except for Florida Power & Light when they won the Deming Prize, no other U.S. companies have yet implemented MBP to a world-class degree.

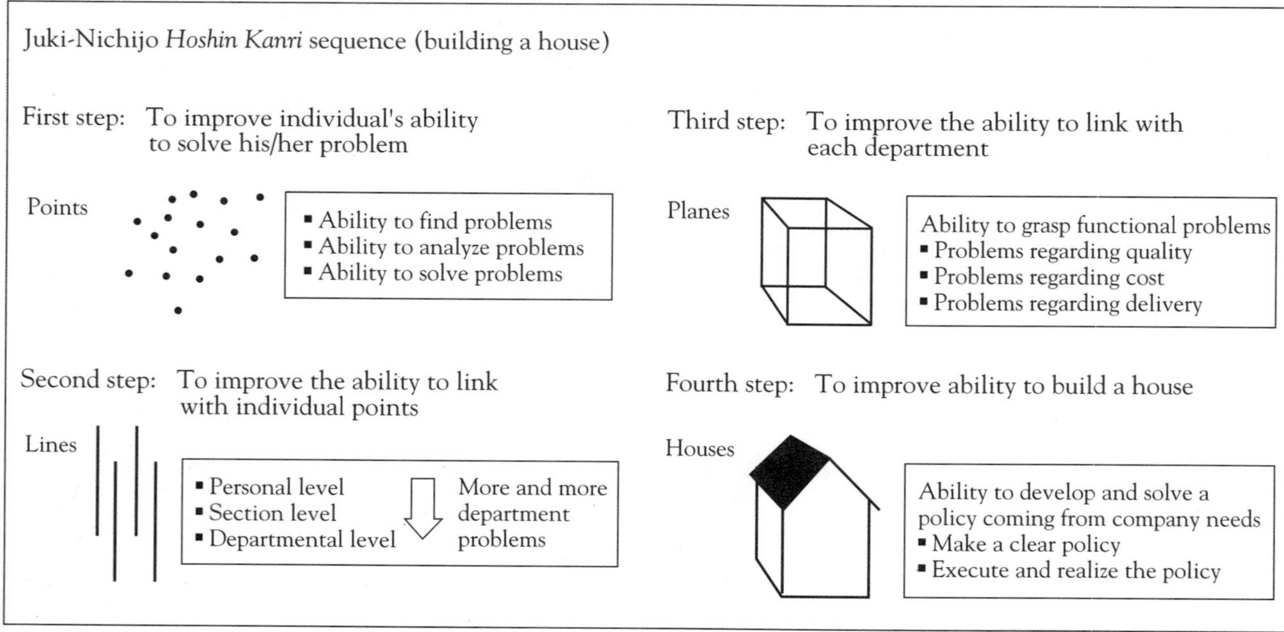

Juki-Nichijo Hoshin Kanri sequence (building a house)
First step: To improve individual's ability to solve his/her problem
Points
▪ Ability to find problems
▪ Ability to analyze problems
▪ Ability to solve problems
Second step: To improve the ability to link with individual points
Lines
▪ Personal level
▪ Section level
▪ Departmental level
More and more department problems
Third step: To improve the ability to link with each department
Planes
Ability to grasp functional problems
▪ Problems regarding quality
▪ Problems regarding cost
▪ Problems regarding delivery
Fourth step: To improve ability to build a house
Houses
Ability to develop and solve a policy coming from company needs
▪ Make a clear policy
▪ Execute and realize the policy

Figure 5.3: Juki's *hoshin kanri* sequence. Steps 2, 3, and 4 resemble DM, CFM, and MBP, respectively.

Most started implementation in the same way that some Japanese companies did—evolving management by objectives into MBP. In fact, most companies started by deploying top management's goals vertically throughout the functional organizations.

Initially there was concern for goals only; means weren't considered. There was little analysis, catchball, or cross-functional coordination, and there were far too many policies (10 to 12). Even so, these companies still feel that they received significant benefits from taking the following initial steps.

1. Considering external and internal customer needs, competitive benchmarking, and the current capability of TQ implementation, in addition to traditional strategic planning inputs
2. Focusing strategic initiatives to a greater degree than before
3. Deploying high-level goals more consistently throughout the organization
4. Implementing an ongoing process to assess TQ implementation, usually using the Malcolm Baldrige National Quality Award criteria

Before initiating MBP to any degree, companies must custom-design its implementation process. An output of this design process is an MBP manual, which is a procedural cookbook for all participants in the process. This manual defines who does what and when, why, and how. The manual documents the process and takes MBP from a merely conceptual level to an operational level. We recommend that the design team be an ongoing team that continually improves the MBP process, evolving it ultimately to the world-class level that we have defined. Ideally, a multiyear strategy and plan to evolve MBP to a world-class level would be a preface to the manual.

Many U.S. companies used this classical sequence of implementation because they were well along on the TQ journey before they heard much about MBP. Since little has been written about

MBP, companies needed to do some digging. Hewlett-Packard, one of the first U.S. companies to initiate MBP implementation, learned about MBP from its Japanese subsidiary, Yokogawa Hewlett-Packard, which won the Deming Prize. Florida Power & Light had the most advanced MBP process in the United States. Figure 5.4 depicts Florida Power & Light's MBP implementation in chronological sequence.

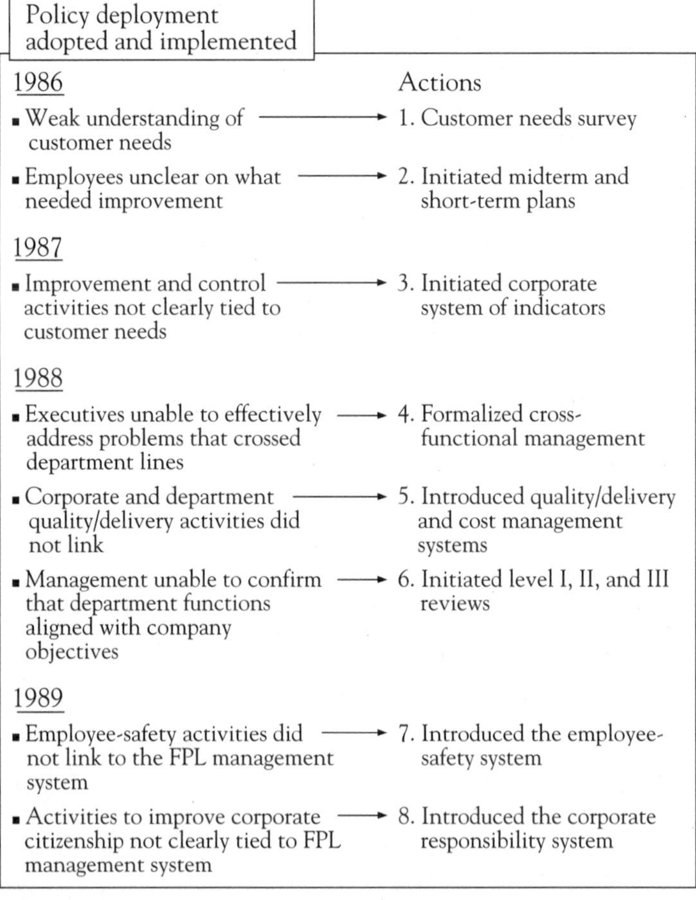

Policy deployment adopted and implemented
1986
Actions
■ Weak understanding of customer needs
1. Customer needs survey
■ Employees unclear on what needed improvement
2. Initiated midterm and short-term plans
1987
■ Improvement and control activities not clearly tied to customer needs
3. Initiated corporate system of indicators
1988
■ Executives unable to effectively address problems that crossed department lines
4. Formalized cross-functional management
■ Corporate and department quality/delivery activities did not link
5. Introduced quality/delivery and cost management systems
■ Management unable to confirm that department functions aligned with company objectives
6. Initiated level I, II, and III reviews
1989
■ Employee-safety activities did not link to the FPL management system
7. Introduced the employee-safety system
■ Activities to improve corporate citizenship not clearly tied to FPL management system
8. Introduced the corporate responsibility system

Figure 5.4: Florida Power & Light's MBP implementation in chronological sequence.

The transition to catchball is a huge step because it requires so much more time than is typically spent in traditional strategic planning efforts. When many companies start, their analysis to determine countermeasures is usually too general; in essence, they're just going through the motions. The catchball process is speeded up considerably when middle- and lower-level managers go through the *establish policy* step independently and concurrently with top management. That is, they develop a draft of what they feel the policies should be along with appropriate countermeasures for the policies. Although their perspective will be different from that of top managers, there will usually be considerable overlap (see Figure 5.5).

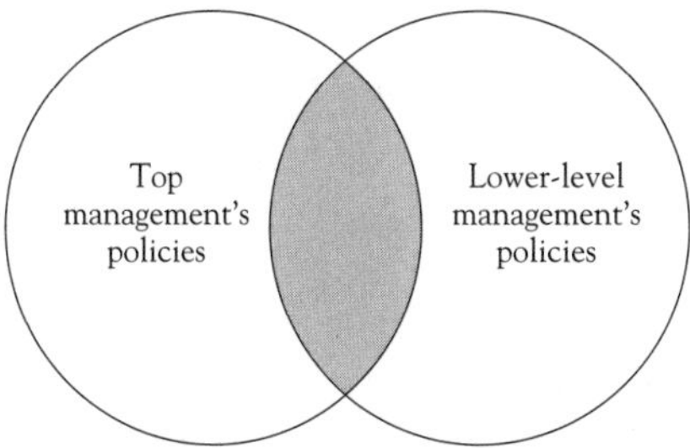

Figure 5.5: The inevitable overlap in the process of establishing policy.

There are several advantages to these parallel activities.

1. Top management benefits from the perspective of lower-level managers.

2. Lower-level managers are better prepared to analyze and respond to top management's draft of policies.

3. Both the duration and total amount of time required for catchball decreases.

Lower-level managers must be adequately informed if they are to develop policy concurrently with top management. Consequently, the overlap between top-management policies and those of other managers increases as the lower levels become better informed about the general business environment (see Figure 5.6).

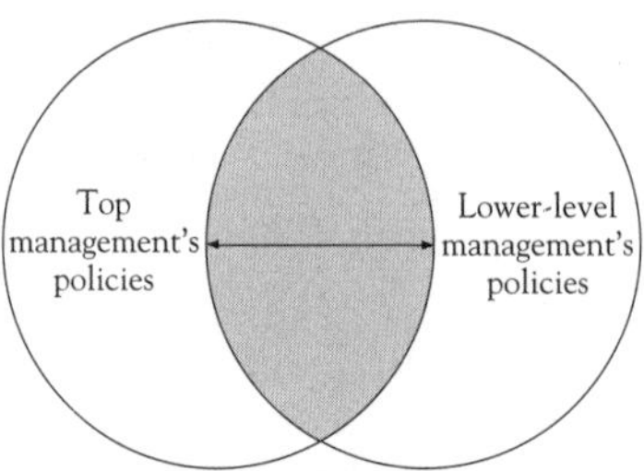

Figure 5.6: The overlap grows as both groups become more informed.

Having frequent reviews of progress relative to the formally approved policies throughout the year helps keep managers well informed. The reviews provide a forum for communication.

A critical requirement for effective catchball is that managers understand the processes for which they are responsible and with which they are involved. To understand means that managers have identified process improvement opportunities.

A Different Approach to Implementation

A number of companies heard about MBP during Phase I of TQ implementation—the awareness phase. Some of these companies have decided to use MBP, to a degree, from the earliest stage of implementation; that is, they identified business objectives and began to use TQ methodology, at least to some degree, to solve those problems. This approach ensures integration of business planning and quality planning, which is a difficult hurdle for many companies.

The first senior management cross-functional committee is typically for quality. This is appropriate because of a fundamental TQ assumption—if the quality system is improved, other good things will happen as a result, such as reduced costs and increased profits. Over time, after TQ implementation is well under way, these companies can add other policies, such as one relating to new product development.

Southern Pacific Transportation Company is one of the companies that started using MBP from the beginning of TQ implementation. After an initial round of TQ awareness they introduced MBP by means of the planning process shown in Figure 5.7.

In its first year Southern Pacific was able to limit its policies to eight high-leverage items. While this is more than the recommended two or three, the process brought focus and provided a framework for achieving rapid improvement. Since it was the first year of TQ implementation, management was just starting to learn process improvement methodology. Therefore, during the first year, people were expected to use only the Pareto chart and cause-and-effect diagram in problem analysis. This got them started using TQ to solve business problems.

Relationship to Strategic Business Planning

The policy development and deployment phases of MBP use a new strategic planning model, shown in Figure 5.8. This model is a combination of the traditional model and nontraditional inputs.

The following scenario is typical of many companies that have implemented TQ. In the early stages of TQ, quality planning is concerned with planning for TQ implementation. Quality is one of many items on the plate, and quality planning is in addition to traditional strategic business planning.

As familiarity with TQ develops, quality becomes a higher-priority issue and some nontraditional inputs begin to be considered in strategic business planning. During this time, quality-related goals begin to account for an increasingly greater percentage of the total

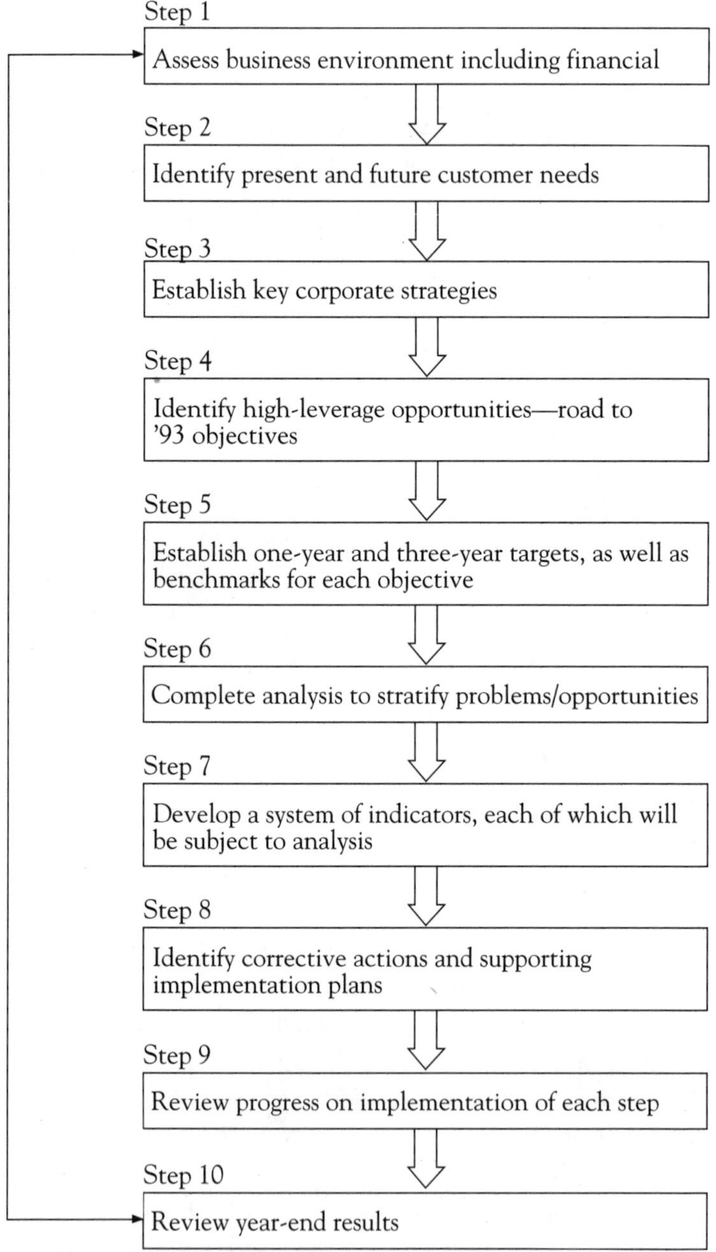

Step 1
Assess business environment including financial
Step 2
Identify present and future customer needs
Step 3
Establish key corporate strategies
Step 4
Identify high-leverage opportunities—road to '93 objectives
Step 5
Establish one-year and three-year targets, as well as benchmarks for each objective
Step 6
Complete analysis to stratify problems/opportunities
Step 7
Develop a system of indicators, each of which will be subject to analysis
Step 8
Identify corrective actions and supporting implementation plans
Step 9
Review progress on implementation of each step
Step 10
Review year-end results

Figure 5.7: Southern Pacific's planning process.

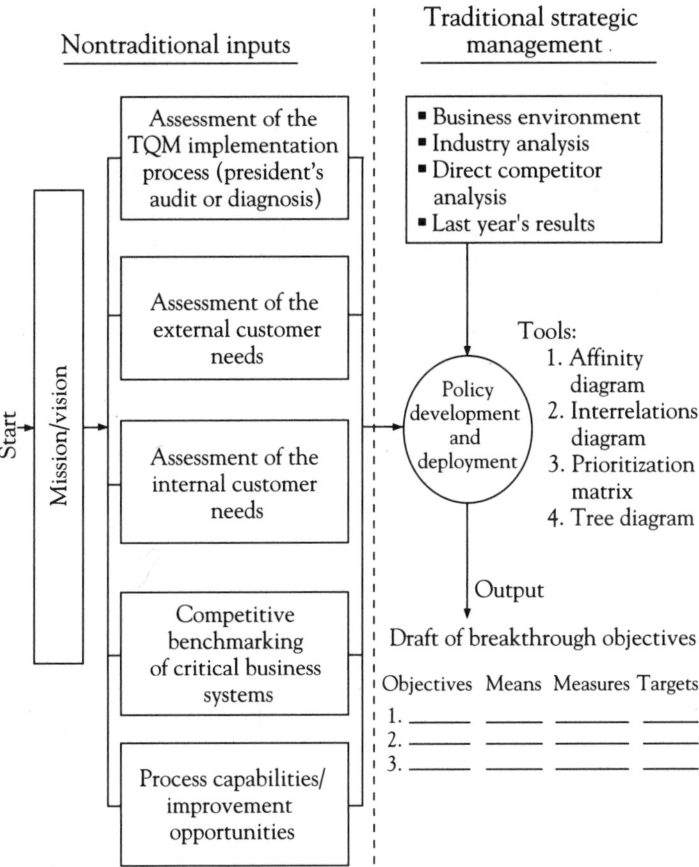

Figure 5.8: The new model for strategic planning is a combination of old and new.

grade on managers' individual performance appraisals. Quality, however, is still viewed as something done in addition to everything else. Quality planning is seen as a part of business planning.

Figure 5.9 depicts this transition. The phases shown correspond to those previously mentioned in the general implementation model. As mentioned previously, integrating quality planning

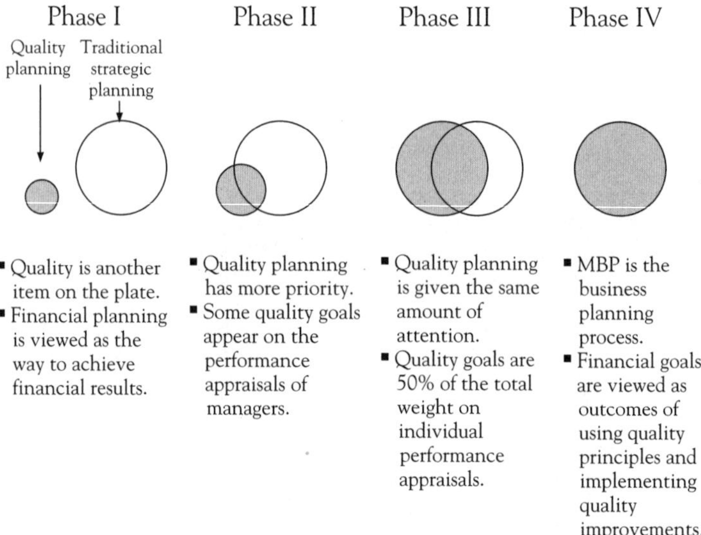

Phase I
Phase II
Phase III
Phase IV
Quality planning
Traditional strategic planning
▪ Quality is another item on the plate.
▪ Financial planning is viewed as the way to achieve financial results.
▪ Quality planning has more priority.
▪ Some quality goals appear on the performance appraisals of managers.
▪ Quality planning is given the same amount of attention.
▪ Quality goals are 50% of the total weight on individual performance appraisals.
▪ MBP is the business planning process.
▪ Financial goals are viewed as outcomes of using quality principles and implementing quality improvements.

Figure 5.9: The transition to MBP as the strategic planning process.

and business planning is greatly facilitated by implementing MBP early in the implementation process.

Given the explanation of fundamentally different MBP implementation approaches and relationship to strategic business planning, we proceed with a discussion of implementation principles.

Implementation Principles

Principle 1. Customize the design of your MBP system

Build upon what currently exists. Evolve your current strategic planning system. To customize the design, assess current capabilities with respect to TQ in general and to elements of MBP specifically. Use the PDCA cycle to design the right implementation system by starting with the *check* step of the cycle. Conduct an organizational assessment of the following items.

General

- Degree of management's TQ understanding
- Degree to which the quality improvement process is practiced, especially cross-functionally

MBP Specific

Establish policy (To what degree are the following in place?)

- Mission
- Vision
- Current strategy/degree of focus
- Customer needs assessment
- Customer satisfaction measurement
- Benchmarking
- Understanding of process capability
- Cross-functional infrastructure
- Current strategic planning process
- Use of the seven basic tools
- Use of the seven new planning tools

Deploy Policy

- Degree of analysis to determine means/countermeasures
- Degree of involvement by those who must execute
- Integration with daily management (DM) system or its equivalent
- Degree of catchball

Implement reviews

- Frequency of reviews
- Review process—judgmental or to seek cause?
- Reviewer identified—who conducts?
- Connection to individual performance review

Implementation Principle 2

Think big in terms of the world-class model of MBP, but implement in small steps. Be certain you can do what you aim to do.

Implementing in small steps with an eye on the final goal—world-class competency—makes change seem more realistic and attainable.

Implementation Principle 3

Communicate openly, comprehensively, and frequently about the business and its environment, the vision, strategy, and plans. Before doing anything else, explain why the company is considering MBP. Present an overview of MBP elements and benefits to all managers. Announce intentions to improve the current strategic planning system by taking advantage of key features of MBP. Next, share an initial draft of a recommendation, including an implementation plan, and obtain feedback. Incorporate this feedback into the final recommendation. Announce the implementation plan.

Pitfalls

Most pitfalls in one way or another relate to not following the previous implementation principles. The most common are

1. Trying to do too much too fast beyond the organization's capability, such as trying at once to implement all elements of the world-class model. Some companies create a paperwork nightmare that becomes just another bureaucratic process and ultimately topples over from its own weight.
2. Insufficient preparation of the organization for a major change.
3. Inadequate planning detail. Lack of planning involvement by those who must execute the implementation plan. Implementing without an MBP manual.
4. Failure to use the PDCA cycle on the implementation process.
5. Lack of understanding of the MBP manual.
6. Not managing the expectations of internal customers; that is, creating the expectation of a world-class model

and implementing a lot less. For example, implementing a version of MBO and calling it MBP.

7. Managers who continue to blame people during the review process instead of helping to diagnose and improve processes.
8. Insufficient analysis to determine means / counter-measures.
9. Lack of an appropriate degree of focus—inability to have only two or three policies.
10. Calling a one-way dictate from top management catchball.

As previously discussed when catchball is initiated, whoever throws the first ball must do it carefully so as not to exceed the ability of the receiver to catch the ball. As the organization's ability to catch the ball increases, the ball can be bigger and can be thrown harder. In fact, the spirit of catchball is that management must throw the ball in such a way as to test the organization's constitution and resiliency. On Japanese flowcharts of MBP systems, a baseball is shown where catchball occurs. In Canon's mature MBP system, the baseball becomes a medicine ball. If it's thrown hard, a medicine ball will certainly test the receiver's fitness.

Finally, we end this chapter with a discussion of one issue that few U.S. companies have seriously addressed. It relates to probably the most sacred of all cows—the individual performance measurement and reward system.

Should MBP Policies Be Tied to Individual Performance Appraisals?

Those who advocate a direct link between the attainment of MBP policies and individual performance appraisals say that it is necessary to motivate individuals sufficiently. Otherwise, they say, people won't do what they need to and/or they won't do it enough. Further, they say, it provides the basis for compensation.

Those who oppose a link between policies and performance appraisals say that it is not needed to motivate; that most people will be motivated sufficiently from buying into the corporate vision and from understanding business realities, especially customer requirements. Further, they feel that individual objectives are counterproductive because they cause people to become internally competitive and to suboptimize their performance at the expense of the whole company. Opponents also contend that it is wrong to hold people accountable for the outcomes of systems over which they don't have total control. This camp believes that the going market rate plus profit sharing, based upon a percentage of regular income, should be used as the basis of individual compensation.

In Japan, there is no direct tie-in between policies and performance appraisals. In the United States, most large companies that are implementing MBP tie policy objectives into performance appraisals, regardless of their degree of TQ implementation.

Although there can be significant quality improvements with a performance measurement appraisal system, we feel that to compete with the TQ masters in the future, most U.S. companies will need to discard it. There are a handful of companies that have discarded performance appraisal as a result of their TQ journey. It's also probably fair to say that most companies that are well along the TQ journey, such as Baldrige Award winners, feel that their current reward systems need to be modified. But in reality all that most have done is to give a greater percentage of the overall evaluation to quality objectives and less to financial objectives. For a more thorough discussion of the implications of TQ on performance measurements and reward systems, see chapter 5 of E. Huge, *Total Quality* (Milwaukee, Wis.: ASQC Quality Press, 1990).

Performance measurements and rewards are one of the key determinants of the organization's culture. The next chapter deals with the issue of creating a culture of involvement, which is probably the most challenging aspect of TQ implementation. Accomplishing a highly participative culture in which decisions are made largely by consensus is especially critical to implementing a world-class MBP capability.

6

Tapping into the Spirit of Management by Policy

The ultimate competitive advantage is a culture which develops the creative energies of all employees better than the competition.

—Akio Morita
Chairman, Sony

Introduction

We've seen a tremendous change in Eastern Europe brought on by economic scarcities and the need for greater personal freedom, involvement, and expression. In the 1990s, quality will be to the U.S. workplace what these massive changes were to Eastern Europe. The spirit or life force of TQ frees the creative energies within all of us.

Management by policy as practiced by Deming Prize-winning companies represents an advanced stage of TQ. Even for some Malcolm Baldrige National Quality Award winners, implementation of world-class MBP requires a significant cultural change! Where does the energy to accomplish such a change come from?

Put succinctly, the answer is to tap into the spirit of TQ. The purpose of this chapter is to explain what this spirit of TQ is and how to tap into its limitless source of energy.

Describing the Spirit

According to Webster, *spirit* is the animating or vital principle held to give life to a concept. It is the life force or energy source.

What, then, is the spirit of TQ? It is the innate need that every person has to

- Work toward a purpose (beyond earning an income)
- Make a difference toward the attainment of that purpose
- Develop his or her capabilities to the fullest
- Be creative
- Have the freedom to be what he or she can be

This is why implementing TQ can be so exciting. It is at the heart of the meaning of quality of life. Without satisfying these needs there can be no quality of work life.

These needs can't be instilled by managers or leaders; they must be tapped into. These needs relate to the highest two tiers of Maslow's hierarchy of needs, shown in Figure 6.1.

These needs can be satisfied only if people are involved in helping the business grow and flourish. Few traditional U.S. companies involve people—including many managers—very much in the business. Therefore, they don't tap into the potential energy that exists. Involvement essentially means that everyone from top management to the front line or shop floor has three jobs.

1. Maintenance—doing the job with the current best practice or at the process standard; that is, controlling the process.

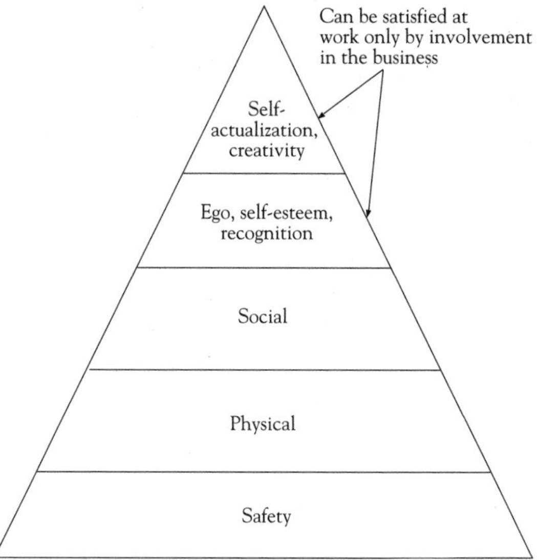

Figure 6.1: Maslow's hierarchy of needs.

2. Improvement—improving the way the job is done; that is, improving the process and advancing the standard.
3. Planning—planning to concurrently maintain and improve the process standard. Involvement of those who must execute the plan in the planning process helps ensure their understanding and commitment to the plan. Behavioral scientists have been saying this for at least 40 years and business schools have been teaching this principle for about as long. Unfortunately, few, if any, U.S. companies have put this principle into widespread practice or deployed it throughout the organization. World-class companies actually do it, and MBP is the system they use.

Previous chapters explained how MBP works. But how does a company transform itself so that every employee can be involved to the degree that we have discussed? How can catchball and the review process take place in the ways we described?

Creating a Culture of Involvement

Leadership sets the tone in an organization by explicit and implicit expectations that follow from its behavior. Therefore, the leadership is key to creating a culture in which all persons are expected, encouraged, and nurtured to be involved. Traditional leadership behavior must change drastically. In fact, the change is so drastic that it is probably more accurate to say that the traditional model needs to be totally discarded and replaced by the new model. There are six drastic behavioral changes that traditional leadership must make.

Change 1. *Leadership must change from commanding and controlling to coaching or facilitating. A commander tells people what to do; a coach helps people to develop their capabilities.* A fundamental assumption of archetypal commanders is that they are smarter than the people they are managing and that they have all the good answers. Commanders don't want to hear about problems because problems imply that they don't have everything in control. They micromanage; that is, they demand unnecessary details to try to catch people without answers. This way they can prove their own superiority and keep people on the defensive. Commanders rule by intimidation.

Coaches realize that they can't know everything that's going on, and that no manager can know as much about each person's job as the person performing it. Coaches make sure that everyone understands the context within which they are working. Good coaches work toward the overall good of the process.

The coach's objective is to build the capability of individuals to further improve the capability of the process to increase customer satisfaction. This is illustrated in Figure 6.2.

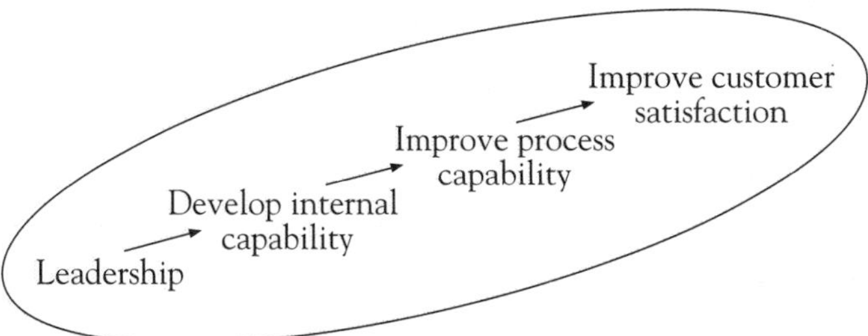

Figure 6.2: Good leadership relates directly to the improvement of customer satisfaction.

Because coaches don't have all the answers, they listen and engage others in a dialogue. This behavior is completely opposite that of the typical commander's one-way communication. Coaches take the pressure off themselves by asking questions to gain understanding. Commanders put pressure on themselves by thinking that they must have all the answers. Good coaches don't blame people when there is a problem; they look to the system instead.

Change 2. *Leadership must change from being internally competitive to cooperative*. The entire management group must work to eliminate all internal competition. These energies must be redirected solely to the external competition. This behavioral change usually requires that management reward systems be changed radically.

Change 3. *Leadership must change from withholding and controlling information to being open and always explaining "why" within the business context*. Commanders withhold information to ensure one-upmanship, control, and superiority. They practice need-to-know communication to the letter because it provides the rationale to withhold information. They are usually cool and unemotional. They hardly ever express their true feelings—unless it's anger at ineptness—because they believe that doing so is a sign of weakness. They rarely admit mistakes.

By comparison, the new leaders are open about their perceptions, always explaining "why," and always explaining the context. A coach operates under the assumption that if people understand the situation, they'll frequently come to the same conclusion or at least understand it. Further, they will be best able to align what they're doing to the needs of the business. Coaches are open about their feelings and encourage the expression of feelings and emotions. They're enthusiastic and celebratory. They are willing to admit their mistakes and view their admission as a vital way to break down barriers that inhibit creative energies and a caring environment.

Without openness, there can be no trust. Without trust there is fear, and people can't do their best. Clearly, leaders must take the first step at being open. Most companies have a long road to travel because they have a long history of shooting the messenger. According to Roger Milliken, chairman of Baldrige Award-winning Milliken, "Instead of shooting the messenger, we must shoot the person who shoots the messenger."

Change 4. *Top management must change from an owner mentality to a trustee mentality*. The traditional attitude is, "I'm the boss. You've got a job to do. Do what I tell you to do and always remember that I'm the boss."

Enlightened leaders views themselves as trustees of the areas they lead. As trustees, they feel obligated to help the area and each individual in it to develop and flourish. Trustees feel responsible for the attitudes that employees have about the company and their jobs.

Trustees feel responsible for peoples' attitudes because they set the environmental tone. They realize that in a short period of time, someone else will become the trustee. Trustees do not feel that they are superior because of their position. They view every person's job as noble and professional.

Change 5. *Leaders must act consistently with their pronouncement that employees are their most valuable asset*. Although most companies say this about their employees, few actually practice it. Essentially, employees are treated as commodities to be laid off during business downturns. Employment security is probably the most pressing concern for all employees, managers as well as nonmanagers. It is also the most important requirement for building a culture of involvement.

Total quality is a superior paradigm because of its focus on customer satisfaction. Thus, increased product demand will be able to absorb the concomitant productivity increases without headcount reductions. Few companies could implement full employment today, but to be true to their pronouncement, leaders must have a long-term vision of employment security for full-time employees and work toward attaining the vision—even if it takes 10 to 15 years to get there. Develop an action plan before business downturns occur. Laying people off must be the last step of the plan. An example of such a plan is as follows:

Step Action

1. Eliminate subcontracting
2. Eliminate temporary help
3. Eliminate part-time employees
4. Eliminate bonuses
5. Make an across-the-board pay cut (same percentage for all employees; managers as well as nonmanagers)
6. Reduce hours
7. Lay offs

In our opinion, paying all persons a large percentage of their income (40 to 50 percent), based upon the company's overall profits, offers the single most significant method of supporting a full employment policy. When there's a business downturn, the profit-sharing bonus reduction will be proportional for all employees and everybody still will be working. Companies won't be able to do this overnight, but they can work toward this point over time.

Change 6. *Leadership must change from controlling to leading by shared vision, values, and beliefs*. Traditional managers overcontrol to a degree that they frequently treat people, including other managers, as children instead of as adults. They see themselves as controllers who must ensure that people do what they're told to do.

The ultimate way to lead is by shared vision, values, and beliefs. If everyone is aligned to the vision, values, and beliefs, control is unnecessary. Alignment provides the control. Leaders who want their company to become world-class must realize that total quality is about a new leadership process. Central to the leadership challenge is that many existing values and beliefs must be changed. This is challenging, but it can be done.

The following is a discussion of three core values/beliefs that must be in place if the previous six behavioral changes are to be made.

Three Fundamental Values/Beliefs

First, leaders must understand that every person has the innate needs identified by Maslow (see Figure 6.1 on page 145). Implicit in this belief is that all persons have untapped creativity and the capability and the will to improve.

Second, leaders must be humble. Without humility, they will continue to be commanders. They won't really listen. Any attempts at listening will come across as patronizing, and will thereby undermine integrity. Humility is required if a manager is to respect people and be receptive to change. *Humility* is a word that neither we nor our colleagues have seen in any philosophy statement of U.S. companies. By contrast, some statement about humility often appears in the operating philosophies of excellent Japanese companies.

Third, leaders must become obsessive about integrity and honesty. They must do what they say they're going to do and behave in a way that is consistent with stated principles. Every decision must be closely scrutinized relative to these principles. Without integrity there can be no trust.

Many companies that have started the quality journey have a philosophy statement that almost always discusses integrity. Tragically, it is often just a word. One of the most widespread breaches of integrity in U.S. businesses is saying that employees are their most important asset.

Companies must take the next step after writing that philosophy statement. They must develop operational definitions of their philosophy statements; that is, they must look at every area of the company and determine what behaviors, conditions, decision criteria, and checkpoints will be needed to ensure that integrity will be maintained. After all, words are only labels. The meaning of the labels in everyday life must be defined. When major decisions are made, the company must explain why this decision is consistent with its principles.

Predictably, the word *trust* also appears in most philosophy statements. When leadership issues a philosophy statement with the words *trust* or *integrity*, they must become extremely sensitive to their implications. Any subsequent act that is inconsistent or unexplained will undermine trust and increase cynicism.

It is vital to understand that there is an even more fundamental belief than integrity. Any attempts to operationalize integrity will be for naught unless there is an absolute, unvarying standard for truth—for what is right and wrong. Since 1989, the Harvard Business School has been trying in vain to teach ethics to the future business leaders of America. Designers of this course have realized that teaching ethics is impossible without absolute standards. Incidentally, the word *ethics* is derived from a Greek word which means *absolute standard*.

Summing Up

Figure 6.3 might help organize the discussion about beliefs and values relative to a culture of involvement within an organization committed to quality. The core beliefs are integrity, humility, and the fact that all persons have value. If the leadership holds these fundamental values and beliefs, it can build a culture of involvement. By using the three management systems (management by policy, cross-functional management, and daily management) to apply the 16 total quality principles, the company can develop the capability for world-class competitiveness.

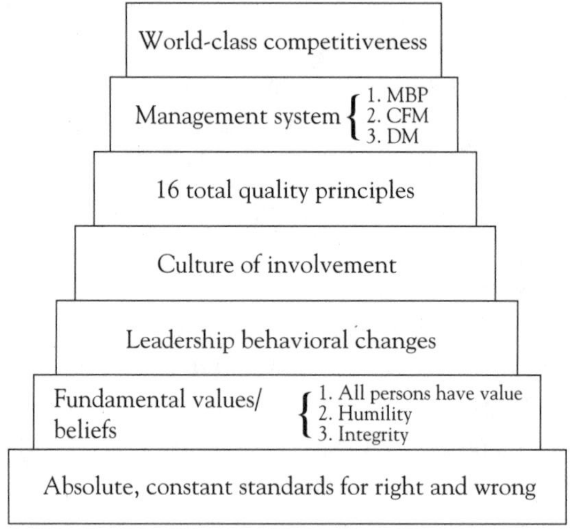

Figure 6.3: Building blocks of world-class competitiveness.

But Nobody's Perfect or Can Be. How Much of This Is Enough to Be a World-Class Competitor?

Deming Award winners, who are masters of the new paradigm of quality improvement, aren't perfect—far from it. But they do practice the fundamental values we've discussed to a much greater degree than their competitors. This gives them a tremendous edge that translates into greater market share and huge profits. Toyota currently has greater liquid assets than the total stock market value of Chrysler and Ford combined.

It's important to note that traditional companies, even before commitment to TQ and a formal effort to implement the 16 TQ principles set forth in chapter 1, can make significant improvements by applying various quality improvement and just-in-time techniques in their existing culture. Such efforts might include robust design, cellular manufacturing, and set-up reduction. These efforts, however, might have little significant employee involvement and a low degree of participative management. And, although world-class MBP requires a very high degree of involvement, significant improvement can be accomplished by implementing just one of the elements of MBP—focusing strategies on only two or three major initiatives. Winning the Deming Prize—which is currently the world's highest recognition for the application of total quality thinking in business—demands both a highly participative environment and a mature MBP system. Figure 6.4 organizes these comparisons.

Conclusion

We live in exciting times. In only a few years the former Soviet Union and Eastern Europe have undergone radical political and social changes that few people, if anyone, thought would happen in this century.

Rapid advances in computer technology are placing more information in the hands of front-line employees and out of the control of middle managers. By empowering nonmanagers with information, computers are helping to push companies toward a culture of involvement. The world's business paradigm has changed from a focus on production to a focus on quality—satisfying customer needs. In response to this new paradigm, great companies have evolved a management system that we feel sets the current world standard.

The purpose of this book is to describe management by policy—the cornerstone of this management system—within the context of total quality.

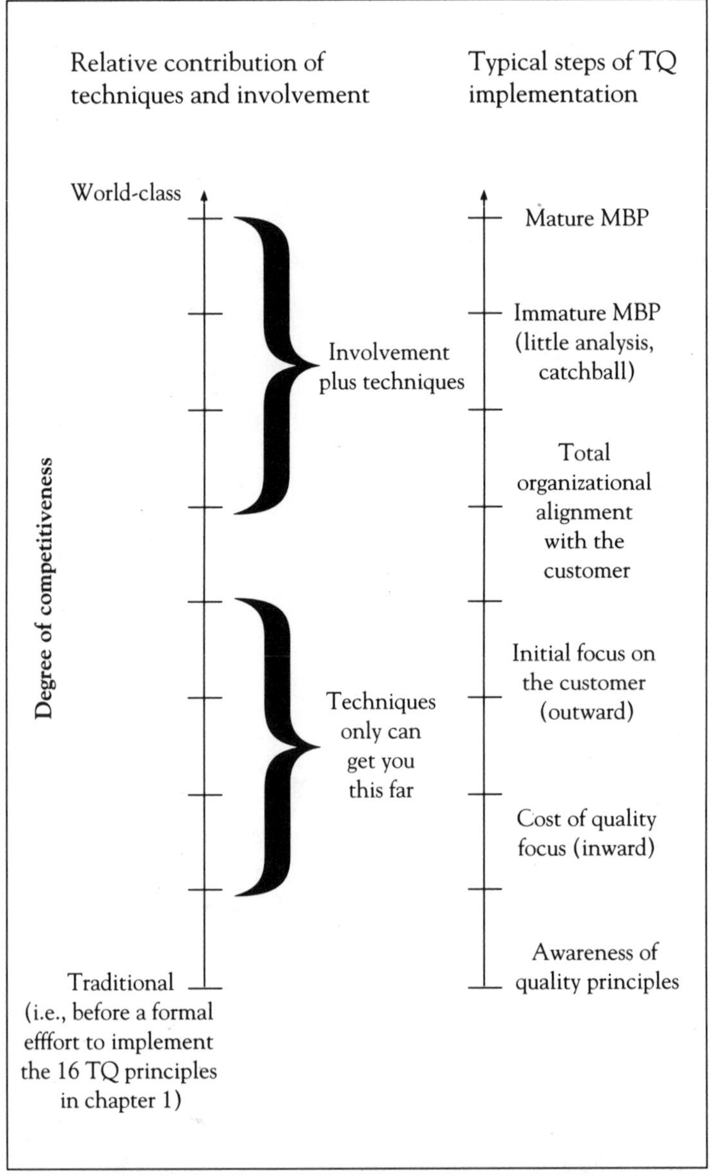

Figure 6.4: Degrees of competitiveness versus TQ implementation stages and relative contribution of techniques and involvement.

Management by policy has the following significant benefits

- Helps develop organizational direction
- Provides a process for changing corporate direction
- Improves the quality of strategic plans
- Allocates resources effectively
- Increases commitment to implementation of strategic business initiatives
- Focuses improvement efforts
- Enhances cooperation
- Develops people better and enhances their understanding of what *world-class* means
- Enhances organizational flexibility
- Connects top management with the front line
- Utilizes TQ principles and emphasizes a quality consciousness
- Improves financial results

Additionally, we discussed implementation issues and suggested ways to implement MBP. As we've described it, MBP represents the most advanced stage of TQ implementation. While we urge full implementation, carrying it to even a modest degree will provide significant benefits.

Most U.S. companies that have set out to implement MBP—ALCOA, American Express Travel Division, AT&T, Blount, DEC, DuPont, Florida Power & Light, Hewlett-Packard, Itel, Procter and Gamble, Southern Pacific Lines, Texas Instruments, some units of Ford and GM, and a few automotive suppliers—feel that it has provided significant advantages.

We appreciate your investment in time to read this book. We hope that it has offered insights that will help you and your company. We wish you the very best in your personal journey of continuous improvement.

Appendix A

Seven Basic Process Improvement Tools

A *flowchart* is used to understand the process and to identify constraints, redundancies, and other non–value-added activities. Similarly, where excessive errors and lead time occur in the process can be determined.

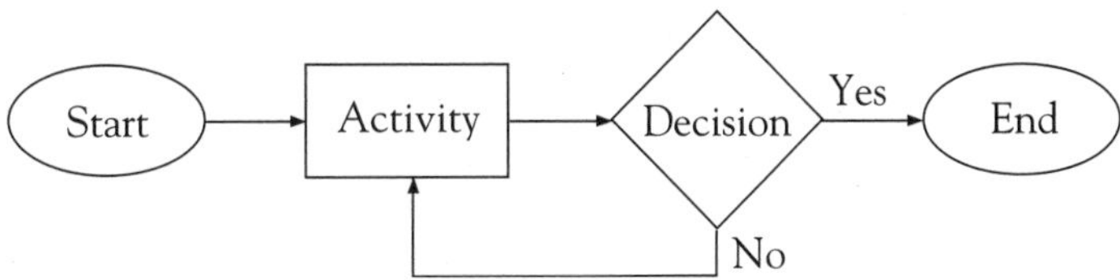

A *cause-and-effect-diagram* organizes potential causes of a desirable or undesirable effect. It assists in identifying root causes by asking, five times, why a cause exists. Development of this tool is credited to Kaoru Ishikawa.

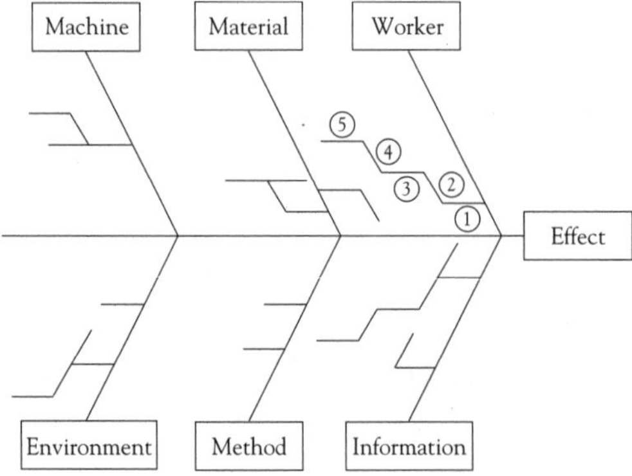

A *Pareto chart* organizes causes by frequency. By using it, the significant few causes that account for most of the effect can be identified.

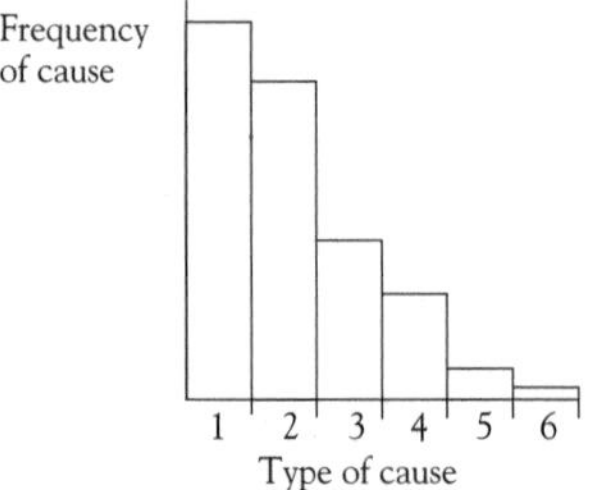

A *scatter diagram* depicts the relationship between variables. Thus, it helps to substantiate whether a potential root cause is related to the effect.

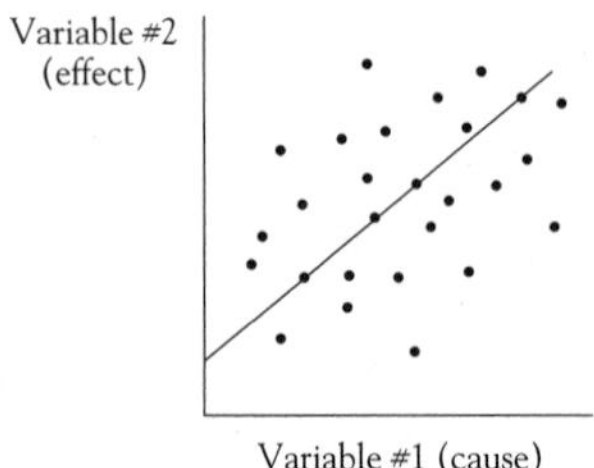

A *histogram* depicts variation. It shows the frequency of occurrence of different measurements for a given quality attribute.

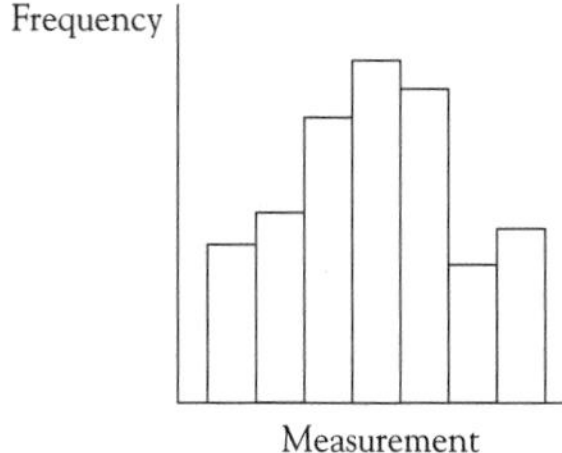

A *run chart* plots data over time. It can also be used to determine whether variation in the data is due to common or special causes by observing variation around the median (that is, the middle value of data that is rank ordered). In the example, data appear to vary randomly around the median. Note: If the data are discrete, then using the median is appropriate. If data are continuous, use the mean.

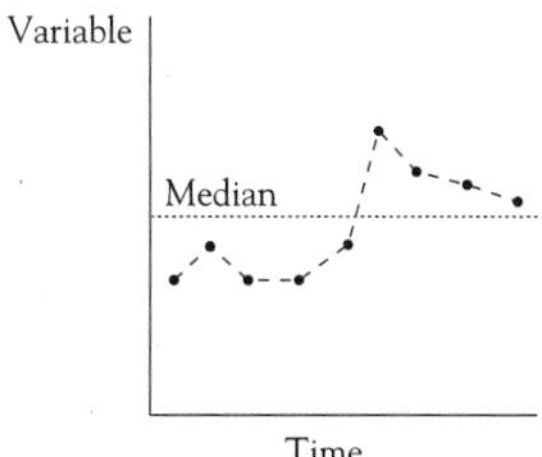

A *control chart* shows whether variation is due to common or special causes. Upper and lower control limits are easily calculated using the averages and ranges of the data observed. Control charts are used only to determine the nature of variation. They are much more precise than run charts relative to indicating whether variation is due to common or special causes.

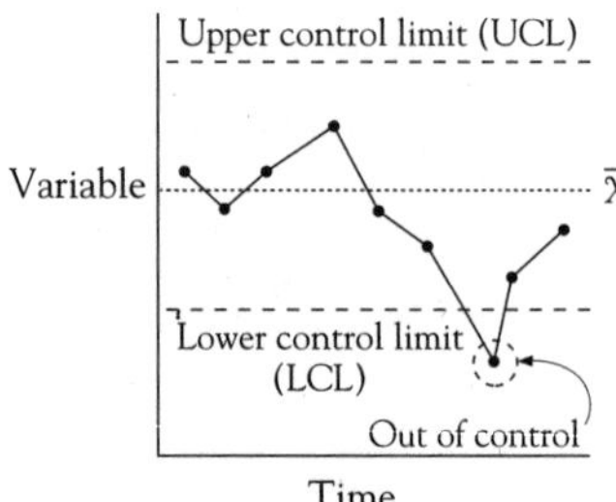
Upper control limit (UCL)
Variable
$\overline{X}$
Lower control limit
(LCL)
Out of control
Time

Appendix B

Seven New Management Planning Tools

For an excellent explanation of the use of the planning tools we recommend Michael Brassard, *The Memory Jogger Plus+*, GOAL/QPC, Methuen, MA, 1989.

An *affinity diagram* (also known as the KJ method) is a team process tool that organizes ideas, generated through brainstorming, into natural groupings in a way that stimulates new creative ideas. Categories and new ideas are obtained by the team members working silently.

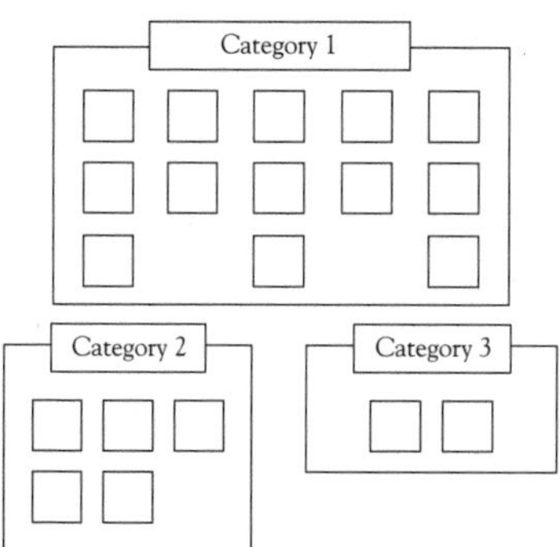

An *interrelationship diagraph* displays the cause-and-effect relationship between factors relating to a central issue. Factors that have a high number of relationships (arrows going into and emanating from) are usually the most fundamental or critical. This diagram shows both the strength (indicated by the boldness of the arrow) and direction.

Central issue

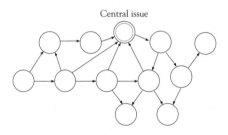

A *tree diagram* shows the complete range and sequence of subtasks required to achieve an objective. A derivative of this tool is fault-tree analysis, which depicts all of the ways that a product or service can go wrong so that preventive measures can be planned.

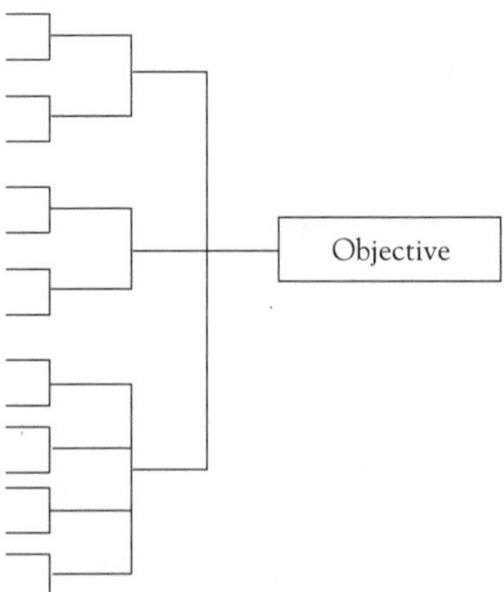

A *matrix diagram* is an excellent way to show the relationships among various data. For example, quality function deployment (QFD) is a process to understand the voice of the customer and to translate it into technical design parameters, subsystems, parts, components, processes, and process controls. The house of quality matrix, used in QFD, is shown. It depicts a tree diagram showing the relationship between primary, secondary, and tertiary customer needs and the technical design parameters or substitute quality characteristics which, if met, would ensure that the customer's needs will be satisfied.

Customer needs			Substitute quality characteristics											
			1				2				3			
Primary	Secondary	Tertiary	a	b	c	d	a	b	c	d	a	b	c	d
A	A.1	A.1.a							△					
		A.1.b		⊙								⊙		
	A.2	A.2.a						○						
		A.2.b			○									△
B	B.1	B.1.a												
		B.1.b				⊙								
	B.2	B.2.a							△		△			
		B.2.b		⊙										
C	C.1	C.1.a										○		
		C.1.b	△						⊙				○	
	C.2	C.2.a										⊙		
		C.2.b												
	C.3	C.3.a			⊙									
		C.3.b	○					△						△

Correlations: ⊙ Strong
○ Moderate
△ Weak

A *prioritization matrix* uses a tree diagram of alternatives and a list of weighted criteria. Prioritization matrices are used to reduce the number of alternatives to those that are most significant in a structured, quantitative way.

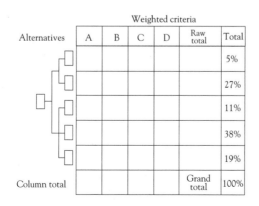

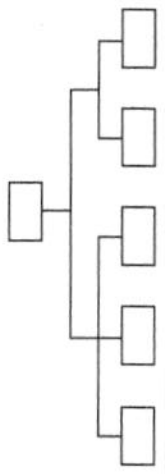

Alternatives	A	B	C	D	Raw total	Total
						5%
						27%
						11%
						38%
						19%
Column total					Grand total	100%

Weighted criteria

A *process decision program chart* (PDPC) is used to plan the implementation of new or revised tasks that are complex. The PDPC maps out all conceivable events that can go wrong and contingencies for these events.

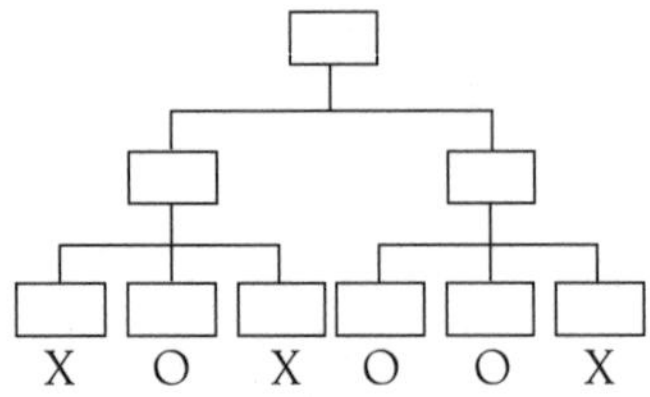

An *arrow diagram* is used to develop the best schedule and appropriate controls to accomplish an objective. It is very similar to the program evaluation review technique (PERT) and the critical path method (CPM).

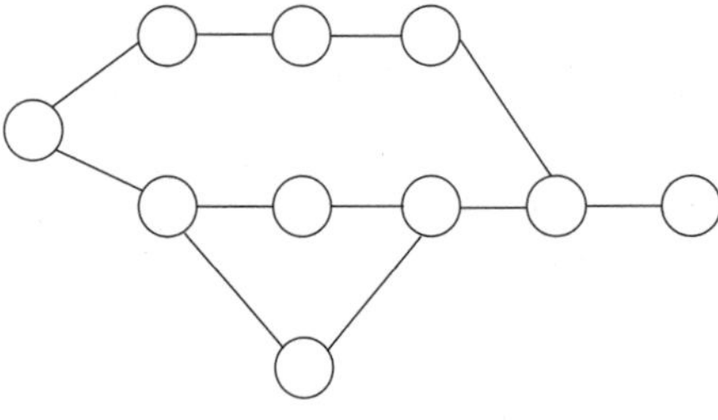

Glossary of Terms

Affinity diagram: One of the seven new management planning tools. It is used to organize ideas into natural groupings in a way that stimulates new creative ideas. Categories and new ideas are obtained by team members working silently so as not to inhibit creativity.

Arrow diagram: One of the seven new management planning tools. It is used to develop the best schedule and appropriate controls to accomplish the schedule. An arrow diagram is similar to the critical path method (CPM) and program evaluation review technique (PERT).

Benchmarking: Involves (1) comparing products and/or services against direct competitors; and (2) comparing critical business processes (such as new product design-to-market process) against the best in the world, regardless of whether or not they are direct competitors. Also called competitive benchmarking.

Catchball: An iterative process of developing objectives and plans to obtain the objectives; sharing them with persons who must execute the plans; requesting and considering their input; and finalizing the objectives and plans after sufficient involvement and commitment from all affected parties.

Cause-and-effect diagram: One of the basic seven process improvement tools. It is used to identify root causes of the effect being analyzed. When possible causes are identified, "Why?" is asked five times to ensure that root causes, not symptoms, are being addressed.

Cellular manufacturing: See just-in-time.

Checkpoint: An upstream process parameter whose variation affects the variation of a process output or control point(s).

Control: Consistently attain or maintain a given process standard. Statistically, it means to eliminate special causes of variation. Also called maintenance. In Japan, control is equivalent to management.

Control chart: Used to determine whether or not variation is due to common or special causes. It is one of the seven basic process improvement tools.

Control point: A process output, such as defects or yield.

Cost of quality: Really the cost of bad quality or of not doing things right the first time. It consists of four major categories.

1. *External failures.* This is the cost associated with correcting a bad product or service when it is with an external customer, for example, warranty expenses or product liability.
2. *Internal failures.* This is the cost of failures or problems that are discovered before products or services leave the company; for example, scrap and rework.
3. *Appraisal.* This is the cost to determine whether or not the products or services are faulty; for example, testing and inspection.
4. *Prevention.* This is the cost associated with any activity whose purpose is to prevent bad quality; for example, training or process improvement teams.

The first three have been termed the *price of nonconformance.*

Countermeasure: The means or method to solve a problem or close the gap between the desired and current states.

Cross-functional management: One of the three major components of the management system of Japanese companies with mature TQ capability. Cross-functional management consists of permanent committees for major processes (such as new product development) and outcomes (such as cost reduction). These committees are comprised of managers representing all major functions. The role of the committees is to plan and ensure the attainment of major cross-functional endeavors to which they are assigned.

DM: See daily management.

DOE: See design of experiments.

Daily management (DM): One of the three major subsystems used by Japanese companies with mature TQ capability. Daily management relates to continuous/incremental process improvement and standardization activities. It involves all persons and includes group process improvement activities as well as individual suggestion systems.

Deming cycle: The same as the plan-do-check-act cycle; also called the Shewhart cycle.

Design of experiments (DOE): A statistical method of designing experiments used in the development and optimization of products and processes. These methods enable product and process designers to find the optimal or nearly optimal design parameters to obtain a robust design without having to test thousands or millions of potential parameter combinations. There are two approaches to DOE: the classical school and the Taguchi methods.

Empowerment: Giving employees the tools (such as knowledge) to eliminate process variation as well as the responsibility, control, and authority for doing so. Further, it means that employees can use their own discretion to exceed the existing job standard if they feel it is required to ensure customer satisfaction.

Facilitator: A resource person required in the implementation of a total quality management system. The primary role of a facilitator is to help the process improvement team leader to lead in the right way, that is, as a coach using the quality improvement process and tools. A facilitator does not get involved in the content of the process improvement team's effort and is concerned only with the team's process to accomplish its objective. If the team leader leads in the right way, a facilitator is not needed.

Fail safing: Designing processes so that they can't go wrong. For example, parts are designed so that they can be assembled only the right way. Called *poka-yoke* by the Japanese.

Five S's: The Japanese approach to ensuring that all persons have the capability and will to do what needs to be done. This process focuses on workplace organization, cleanliness, and standardization.

Flowchart: Used to understand a process by depicting its various activities and decision points. As a result, process constraints, sources of errors and excessive lead time, redundancies, and other non–value-added activities can be identified. It is one of the seven basic process improvement tools.

Gap: The difference between customer expectations and supplier performance.

Goal: Used synonymously with target. See target.

Histogram: A graphic device that depicts variation in an observed measurement. A histogram shows the frequency of occurrence of different measurements for a given quality attribute. It is one of the seven basic process improvement tools.

Hoshin kanri: The Japanese term for management by policy.

Hoshin planning: Another term for management by policy. It is not a good term because the process involves more than planning.

Improvement: Statistically, it means to reduce variation due to common causes (that is, inherent variation of the process). There are two categories of improvement: (1) *Kaizen*—incremental improvements (that is, many, small, frequent, and continuous); and (2) *Innovation*—infrequent, major, large, and quantum-level improvements. Innovation categories, such as those used by Blount, are shown.

Blount's Hierarchy of Innovation

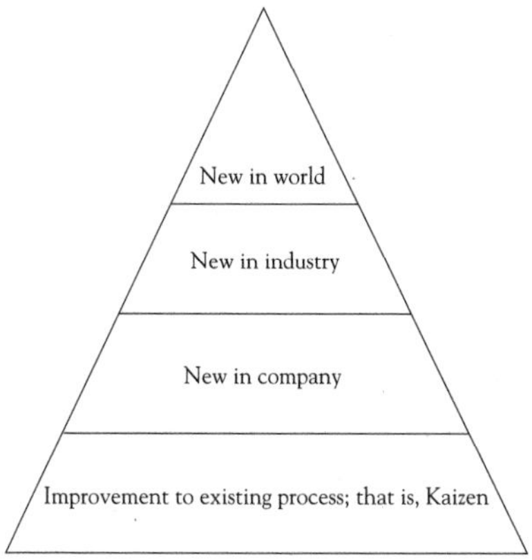

New in world

New in industry

New in company

Improvement to existing process; that is, Kaizen

Indicator: A measurement.

Innovation: A category of improvement. See improvement.

Inspection at the source: People performing an operation are accountable for the quality of their work and inspect their work. Contrasts with a traditional approach whereby another person inspects the work.

Integration: A frequently used term in the Malcolm Baldrige National Quality Award criteria. As such, it means compatible, complementary improvement efforts and cross-functional initiatives relative to a strategic quality plan.

Integration is not a traditional financial plan with some quality-related objectives. It is a system for concurrent improvement and maintenanace activities. It operates at a level where quality initiatives provide competitive advantage. Integration is consistent with a company's mission and vision. It is streamlined so that the necessary workforce and budget follow from the quality improvement initiatives.

Interrelationship digraph: Displays the relationships between factors in a complex situation. It is one of the new management planning tools.

Involvement: All employees are expected to have three jobs.

1. Doing their job
2. Improving the way their job is done
3. Contributing to plans that they must execute

Jidoka: A Japanese term meaning a process designed to stop automatically when there is a problem.

Just-in-time (JIT): A production system and philosophy that was developed by Toyota over a 25-year period. JIT and total quality are like two sides of the same coin; world-class JIT requires world class total quality. The following are attributes of a JIT production system that are required in addition to total quality principles.

1. *Short set-up times* (less than ten minutes), which allow small lot sizes and short lead times.
2. *Cellular manufacturing*, which arranges production processes so that families of similar parts can be produced with minimal queues between operations.
3. *Workplace organization*, which means having a place for everything and everything in its place, clean and ready for use.
4. *Total productive maintenance*, which is an approach whose aim is zero machine breakdowns by improving the capability and reliability of equipment and involving equipment operators in improvement activities.
5. *Balanced operations*—so that all operations take about the same time. A corollary to this principle is to go only as fast as the slowest operation in order not to build an inventory.
6. *Doing a little of everything every day* instead of manufacturing in large lots infrequently.
7. *Pull production system*, which essentially means to build to an order or to an authorization from the customer operation.
8. *Shop floor control by sight* instead of complex computer systems. World-class JIT systems require from one-tenth to one-fiftieth the inventory of traditional manufacturing systems and, therefore, don't need complex systems to keep track of inventory.

JUSE: Japanese Union of Scientists and Engineers.

Kaizen: A category of improvement. See improvement.

Kanban: In Japanese, it literally means *card*. Used in pull production systems to either authorize an operation to produce or move parts.

MBO: See management by objectives.

MBP: See management by policy.

Maintenance: Relative to process improvement and control, it is synonymous with process control, that is, maintaining a process at its current standard.

Management by objectives (MBO): Traditional Western management approach whereby management specifies organizational objectives (usually financial results) and holds individuals accountable for their attainment without analysis or an understanding of the processes that produce the results.

Management by policy (MBP): One of three major components of the management system used by Japanese companies with mature TQ capability. Management by policy determines the key organizational objectives and means to obtain the objectives, deploys them throughout the entire organization, and makes regular reviews to ensure that the objectives are met and the means are followed. Also called policy management, policy deployment, *hoshin kanri*, and *hoshin* planning.

Management by process: New management approach in which the focus is on improving the process with an eye on results.

Matrix diagram: Shows the relationships among various data including the relative strength. It is one of the seven new management tools.

Mission: Why an enterprise exists; its *raison d'etre* and the scope of the business it's in. For example, Exxon's mission could be oil energy or a financial conglomerate.

Objective: Specifically refers to a desired result. In the context of MBP, a policy is comprised of both an objective and the means to accomplish the objective.

Operating philosophy: A statement of fundamental values, beliefs, assumptions, credo, philosophy, and principles.

Pareto chart: Organizes causes by frequency so that a significant few causes, which may account for most of the effect, can be identified. Also known as the 80/20 rule; that is, 80 percent of the effect is due to 20 percent of the causes. It is one of the seven basic process improvement tools.

PDCA: See plan-do-check-act.

PDPC: See process decision program chart.

PON: See price of nonconformance.

Plan-do-check-act (PDCA) cycle: Also called the Deming cycle or Shewhart (original developer) cycle. It is the application of the scientific method to process control and improvement. Essentially, it means to analyze a situation or process; decide on an alternative and plan its implementation; implement the alternative; determine whether it worked; if so, institutionalize it; if not, discard it and try again. Recently, Dr. Deming refers to this cycle as the plan-do-study-act cycle.

Poka-yoke: The Japanese term for fail safing.

Policy: In management by policy and in the Deming Prize checklist, *policy* means the overarching or key objectives for the organization and the means by which the objectives are obtained.

Policy management: See management by policy.

Prevention-based process/system to ensure quality: Can be contrasted to a system based upon inspection, which is reactive. A prevention-based system identifies those upstream activities which, if done, ensure that the results will be satisfactory. A prevention-based system is proactive.

Price of nonconformance (PON): See cost of quality.

Prioritization matrices: Used to determine the highest-priority options or alternatives relative to accomplishing an objective. It is one of the seven new planning tools.

Problem: A gap between what is desired by the customer and what currently exists.

Problem-solving tools: The seven basic process improvement tools.

1. Flowchart
2. Cause-and-effect diagram
3. Pareto chart
4. Histogram
5. Scatter diagram
6. Run chart
7. Control chart

See Appendix A for a description of each tool.

Process: All of the activities, people, machines, information, material, measurements, and methods required to accomplish a task.

Process capability: The inherent variation of a process relative to the variation that is acceptable to the customer. That is, if the inherent variation is very small relative to the customer needs and the process is centered at or near the target, then the process is said to be highly capable.

Process decision program chart (PDPC): Identifies all events that can go wrong and the appropriate countermeasures for these events.

Pull production system: A production approach whereby material isn't moved or produced until a signal is received from the customer operation. It contrasts with a traditional push system whereby material is produced to a centrally developed schedule (such as material requirements planning) and pushed to the next operation or the stockroom whether or not the customer operation needs it.

QIP: See quality improvement process.

Quality: Good quality results from the customer's perception that expectations have been met or exceeded. With respect to customer satisfaction, perception is reality. Customers are both internal and external to the business. External customers include the ultimate end users and hierarchy of companies between the company and end users.

Quality circles: Natural work units (unifunctional) that meet regularly to improve quality. Typically, quality circle members are volunteers. The circle usually determines what it is going to address. Quality circles contrast with process improvement teams, which are typically multifunctional and work on issues that are specified by management.

Quality function deployment (QFD): A process to understand the voice (expectations) of the customer and to translate the customer's voice into technical design parameters (substitute quality characteristics), subsystems, parts, components, processes, and process controls.

Quality improvement process (QIP): Includes the following steps: (1) identify the customer; (2) understand customer needs; (3) determine gaps between customer's perception of delivered product and/or service and expectations; (4) identify the processes causing the gaps; and (5) apply the PDCA cycle and the seven basic quality tools to improve the process and close the gaps. Quality improvement is a never-ending cycle to design a new standard, maintain control around the standard, and then reduce variation.

Quality of conformance to design: The degree to which the delivered product or service quality reflects the intended quality of design.

Quality of design: The degree to which the intended product or service design satisfies the customer's needs for a designated market area.

Robust design: A design that is relatively insensitive to the variation in customer usage, production processes, material, and components.

Run chart: Plots data over time (for example sales per month). It is one of the seven basic process improvement tools.

SDCA: See standardize-do-check-act cycle.

Scatter diagram: Depicts the relationship between variables, thereby helping to substantiate whether or not a potential root cause is related to the effect. It is one of the seven basic process improvement tools.

Seven new planning tools for management: These are as follows:

1. Affinity diagram (also called the KJ method)
2. Interrelationship digraph
3. Tree diagram
4. Matrix diagram
5. Prioritization matrices
6. Process decision program chart (PDPC)
7. Arrow diagram

See Appendix B for a description of each tool.

Shewhart cycle: Also known as the Deming cycle or the plan-do-check-act cycle. See plan-do-check-act cycle.

Standard: The current best practice for an activity or process.

Standardization: The process by which all persons follow the current standard. Management's job is to ensure standardization. When a process is improved, doing all of the things required to ensure that the improvement is institutionalized (that is, used pervasively in the company), and that the gains are sustained. Standardization means the same as *maintenance*.

Standardize-do-check-act (SDCA) cycle: A variation of the PDCA cycle, whereby the *P* step entails planning to replicate a process standard throughout an organization.

Statistical process control: Using a statistical control chart to monitor a process to determine the nature of its variation. Based upon the nature of variation, a decision is made to leave the process alone or to take appropriate action. Any actions will utilize the quality improvement process.

Statistical thinking: This is the means to understand variation in all processes and the implications of the nature of variations. Dealing with special causes of variation requires one strategy, whereas common causes requires another strategy.

Storyboarding: The process of documenting the application of the quality improvement process (QIP) to a specific area or process. Ideally, the QIP will be displayed prominently on a board or wall to make it as visible as possible. The term originated with Walt Disney, who used to display ideas and issues prominently to enhance communication and to make it easy for people to contribute ideas.

Stratification: Breaking down the whole into smaller related parts. For example, data about the U.S. population can be stratified by age, sex, occupation, race, ethnic group, and so on. Stratification is vital in analysis because significant differences can exist for various parts of the whole.

System: A group of processes that together accomplish a specific purpose.

Target: A specific end result by a given time. Comparing target with objective: an objective is to improve billing accuracy, and a target is to reduce errors to .01% by December 1993.

TQM: See total quality.

Total productive maintenance: A continuous improvement approach that is focused on equipment. Its aim is zero breakdowns through improved process capability and reliability. Involving equipment operators in the maintenance process and continually upgrading their capability to do more complex maintenance is a fundamental component of this improvement approach. Preventing breakdowns through robust processes is another key ingredient.

Total quality (TQ): Sometimes referred to as total quality management (TQM). An organizational philosophy committed to meeting or exceeding customer's needs through continuous improvement of business processes resulting from the continuous development of people's capabilities.

Tree diagram: Shows the complete range of subtasks required to achieve an objective. It is one of the seven new management tools.

Value engineering: Also called value analysis or VA/VE. This improvement methodology was originated by Lawrence Miles of General Electric in the 1940s. This approach focuses on the end uses or function of the product or service being studied rather than its component parts. The worth to the customer and the cost are determined for each function. Value is defined as the worth to the customer divided by cost. Where functions have an imbalance between worth to customer and cost, other design concepts are considered that can provide the same function at a lower cost. Although many U.S. businesses and the Department of Defense started value engineering equivalent programs, most have been abandoned. Those that still exist seem to exist only in pockets within companies. Seldom are they companywide standard operating procedures. By contrast, the procedure is used pervasively by many Japanese companies. These companies use value engineering to ensure customer satisfaction at the lowest cost.

Vision: A picture of the future state of the business in five, ten, or 20 years. Such a vision provides direction for strategic planning, the purpose of which is to attain the vision. An example of a vision statement is to be the recognized world leader in financial services. Visions can be more comprehensive and can define how things will work relative to different categories, such as the following:

- Customers
- Leadership
- Information and analysis
- Strategic quality planning
- Process and process assurance
- Human resource utilization

Bibliography

Akao, Yoji, ed. *Hoshin Kanri: Policy Deployment for Successful TQM*. Cambridge, Mass.: Productivity Press, 1991.

Andrews, Don. "Hoshin Planning." In *GOAL/QPC Conference Notes*. Methuen, Mass.: GOAL/QPC, 1989.

Ashburn, Tom. "Hoshin Kanri: The Orchestration of Continuous Improvement." In *GOAL/QPC Conference Notes*. Methuen, Mass.: GOAL/QPC, 1988.

Block, Peter. *The Empowered Manager: Positive Political Skills at Work*. San Francisco: Jossey-Bass, 1988.

Brassard, Michael. "MBP Key Questions to be Addressed." In *GOAL/QPC Conference Notes*. Methuen, Mass.: GOAL/QPC, 1988.

———. *Memory Jogger Plus+™*. Methuen, Mass.: GOAL/QPC, 1989.

Brunetti, Wayne. "Policy Deployment—A Corporate Road Map." Wilton, Conn.: Juran Institute, 1986.

DeFail, Anthony. "Using Hoshin Planning to Implement Total Quality Improvement." In *GOAL/QPC Conference Notes*. Methuen, Mass.: GOAL/QPC, 1991.

Deming, W. Edwards. *Out of the Crisis*. Cambridge, Mass.: MIT Center for Advanced Engineering Study, 1986.

DePree, Max. *Leadership Is an Art*. East Lansing, Mich.: Michigan State University Press, 1987.

Edson, Jim, and Robert Shannahan. "Managing Quality Across Barriers." *Quality Progress* (February 1991): 45–48.

Fowler, Theodore. *Value Analysis*. New York: Van Nostrand, 1990.

Fuller, Tim. "Achieving The Corporate Vision Through Policy Deployment—Cornerstone of Total Quality Management." In *GOAL/QPC Conference Notes*. Methuen, Mass.: GOAL/QPC, 1989.

Galgano, Alberto. "Policy Deployment and Quality Function Deployment in Italy." In ASQC *Annual Quality Congress Transactions*. Milwaukee, Wisc.: ASQC, 1990.

Garvin, David A. *Managing Quality*. New York: Free Press, 1988.

GOAL/QPC. "Daily Process Management: A Research Committee Briefing." In *GOAL/QPC Conference Notes*. Methuen, Mass.: GOAL/QPC, 1990.

GOAL/QPC Research Committee. "Cross-Functional Management." Methuen, Mass.: GOAL/QPC, 1991.

———. "Hoshin Planning: A Planning System for Implementing Total Quality Management (TQM)." In *GOAL/QPC Conference Notes*. Methuen, Mass.: GOAL/QPC, 1989.

Gold, Lois. "Implementing Hoshin and Daily Management in an Area Sales Module." In *GOAL/QPC Conference Notes*. Methuen, Mass.: GOAL/QPC, 1989.

Gunter, Berton. "A Perspective on the Taguchi Methods." *Quality Progress* (June 1987): 44–52.

Hall, Robert W. *Attaining Manufacturing Excellence*. Homewood, Ill.: Dow Jones-Irwin, 1987.

Hewlett-Packard. "An Introduction to Hoshin Kanri." 1991.

Huge, Ernest C. *Total Quality*. Homewood, Ill.: Business One Irwin, 1990.

Imai, Masaaki. *Kaizen: The Key to Japan's Competitive Success*. New York: Random House, 1986.

Ishikawa, Kaoru. *What Is Total Quality Control? The Japanese Way*. Englewood Cliffs, N.J.: Prentice Hall, 1985.

Japan Management Association. *Canon Production System*. Cambridge, Mass.: Productivity Press, 1987.

Johnson, H. Thomas. *Relevance Regained*. New York: Free Press, 1992.

Juran, Joseph M. *Juran on Leadership for Quality*. New York: Free Press, 1989.

———. *Juran on Quality by Design*. New York: Free Press, 1992.

JUSE Problem Solving Research Group. *TQC Solutions Vol. II*. Cambridge, Mass.: Productivity, 1991.

King, Bob, and Joe Colletti. "Report on GOAL/QPC Hoshin Planning. Japan Study Mission, July 1, 1991." Methuen, Mass.: GOAL/QPC, 1991.

King, Bob. *Hoshin Planning: The Developmental Approach*. Methuen, Mass.: GOAL/QPC, 1989.

Kogure, Masao. "Some Fundamental Problems on Hoshin-Kanri in Japanese TQC Around Current Concepts on Management by Policy Deployment in Most TQC Applying Companies." In *ASQC Annual Quality Congress Transactions*. Milwaukee, Wis.: ASQC, 1990.

Koura, Kozo. "Survey and Research in Japan Concerning Cross-Functional Management." Unpublished manuscript.

———. "Survey and Research in Japan Concerning Policy Management." In *ASQC Annual Quality Congress Transactions*. Milwaukee Wisc.: ASQC, 1990.

———. "System of Management by Policy." In *International Congress on Quality Control Conference Proceedings*. Tokyo: ICQC, 1987.

Kumar, Sanjoy, and Yash Gupta. "Cross-Functional Teams Improve Manufacturing at Motorola's Austin Plant." *Industrial Engineering* (May 1991): 32–35.

Miyauchi, I. "Management by Policy." Tokyo: Japanese Union of Scientists and Engineers, 1990.

Mizuno, Shigeru. "Policy Management and Cross-Functional Management." In *Companywide Total Quality Control*. Tokyo: Asian Productivity Organization, 1988.

Monden, Y. *Cost Management in the New Manufacturing Age*. Cambridge, Mass.: Productivity Press, 1992.

Monden, Y., and M. Sakuri, eds. *Japanese Management Accounting*. Cambridge, Mass.: Productivity Press, 1989.

Moran, J. W., C. Collett, and C. Cote. *Daily Management: A System for Individual and Organizational Optimization*. Methuen, Mass.: GOAL/QPC, 1991.

Morita, Akio. *Made in Japan*. New York: Dutton, 1986.

Nakajima, Sciichi. *Total Productive Maintenance*. Cambridge, Mass.: Productivity Press, 1988.

Nayatani, Y. *Management by Policy for Promotion of TQC Through Utilization of New QC 7 Tools* (in Japanese). Tokyo: Japanese Union of Scientists and Engineers, 1982.

Osada, Hiroshi. *Management by Policy (Hoshin Kanri)*. 1989.

Osada, Takashi. *The 5 S's: Five Keys to a Total Quality Environment*. Tokyo: Asian Productivity Organization, 1991.

Ozawa, Masayoshi. *Total Quality Control and Management: The Japanese Approach*, 45–56. Tokyo: JUSE Press, 1991.

Scholtes, Peter R. *The Team Handbook*. Madison, Wis.: Joiner Associates, 1988.

Shingo, Shigeo. *A Revolution in Manufacturing: The SMED System*, Stamford, Conn.: Productivity, 1985.

———. *Zero Quality Control: Source Inspection and the Poka-Yoke System*. Stamford, Conn.: Productivity, 1986.

———. *Nonstock Production*. Stamford, Conn.: Productivity, 1988.

Sullivan, Lawrence P. "Policy Management Through Quality Function Deployment." *Quality Progress* (June 1988): 18–20.

Taguchi, Genichi. *Introduction to Quality Engineering*. Tokyo: Asian Productivity Organization, 1986.

"Ten Things List: Key to Cross-Functional Success." *Total Employee Involvement* (February 1990): 1–3.

Tersteeg, Doug. "Hoshin Planning at Zytec." In GOAL/QPC *Conference Notes*. Methuen, Mass.: GOAL/QPC, 1991.

Voehl, Frank W. "Hoshin Kanri, American Style." *Quality Digest* (October 1991): 31–36.

Walden, James C. "Integrating Customer Satisfaction into Daily Work." Wilton, Conn.: Juran Institute, 1986.

Zeithaml, V., A. Parasuraman, and L. Berry. *Delivering Service Quality*. New York: Free Press, 1990.

Index